Yesterday Children

BIDFORD-ON-AVON REMEMBERED

Rodney Crompton, Mike Gerrard,
Roger Leese, Sandra Parker,
Mark Shaddick, Wendy Shaddick

BIDFORD AND DISTRICT HISTORY SOCIETY

'O, call back yesterday, bid time return.'

Richard II, William Shakespeare
(Act III, Scene ii)

Bidford Publications

I HAVE JUST ARRIVED AT BIDFORD

© Bidford and District History Society
Published by Bidford Publications
2013
ISBN 978-0-9575790-0-2

Designed by Matthew Lloyd   www.thinkgraphic.co.uk
Printed by Butler Tanner & Dennis   www.butlertanneranddennis.com

CONTENTS

FOREWORD

As a former Bidfordian, I am pleased that the Bidford History Society has taken this initiative and recorded so much of the social and human history of the village during the century in which we all grew up. I have been impressed by the recollections of the contributors and the narrative put together by the authors, which combine to form a very interesting account of a resilient community in an era of non-stop change. The love and pride shining through the story are their own witness to the achievements of Bidford and its people during our own life time.

I was born in a mining community in Wales in November 1945. My father Frederick Langford was seriously injured in the war, forcing him to spend a year and a half in hospital in Brecon. He later became a manager at the Llanharan Co-op in Glamorgan and in 1947 was appointed 'executive' for all the Bidford Co-op shops.

Between 1947 and 1957 we grew fond of Bidford. We went to Wales for our holidays and I loved the mountain countryside, which was quite different from the thriving community of Bidford. But there were things in common: for example, post-war rationing was exactly the same in the two villages.

My father enjoyed life in Bidford, playing cricket, and learning much that was new to him. He was fascinated by the Anglo-Saxon burials behind the Co-op, and found the grey stone of the buildings at the heart of the village very striking. My mother Myrtle stayed at home, except at weekends, when she went shopping in Birmingham or made visits into the Cotswolds.

Dealing with farmers and nurserymen was a significant change for both of my parents. They made friends with Mr Tyas and his wife who lived close-by, and my mother let me visit Mr Trayford's strange, green wooden dwelling with its green roof, where he gave me the forbidden treat of Ginger Nut biscuits. I grew bolder, wandering down the footpath past the Methodist church and through the village as far as the Bridge.

In 1950 I went to the Infant School close to our house in Victoria Road. I was delighted with many things about the Infant School. I was given 'The Children of the Tump' as a prize and still have it to this day. As my teacher observed, I was different from the other children, dark, and with a Welsh character and language, but I was becoming more accustomed to Englishness and Anglo-Saxon characteristics, especially the blonde hair of the girls. I was still cautious, and watched from afar the group of children who always seemed to be at the centre of activities. I did make friends, especially one in my year from the Locke family.

Over the years I have continued to visit the village from time to time. Although I was there for just ten years of my childhood, I have never really lost my feeling for Bidford. The memories I laid down when a child have stayed vividly with me throughout my life.

Paul Langford
Professor of Modern History,
University of Oxford, 1996-2012

ACKNOWLEDGEMENTS

The idea for the book emanated from discussions within the Committee of the Bidford and District History Society, which, under its Chairman, John Alexander-Head, has given continuing support and encouragement to the research team. The interviews, research and the writing of the book have been a collaborative effort and the team accepts collective responsibility for any errors and for the views expressed.

The team especially wishes to acknowledge the generous financial support from the following: the Stratford-upon-Avon Community Development Fund, without which the publication of the book would not have been possible; Bidford and District History Society; Bidford-on-Avon Parish Council; and Bidford-on-Avon Community Group.

Thanks are also due to: Mary Alexander-Head, Elizabeth Barry, Christine Broughton, Jane Hall, Jane Hosell and Judy Smith for transcribing the interviews; John Alexander-Head and John Cole for their helpful comments as Readers; Lorna Edwards for undertaking the onerous task of proof reading and Jane Crompton for correcting early drafts; Heather Gerrard for assisting with the interviews; Gabrielle Leese and Richard Parker for their contributions to the research; Shelagh Murray for making available her father's manuscript memoirs; and the numerous people who gave permission for their photographs and postcards to be used in the book.

The team is particularly grateful to its editorial consultant, Harvey Woolf, for his constructive suggestions and unfailing encouragement throughout the writing process, and to Professor Paul Langford for agreeing to write the Foreword. It is also indebted to Matthew Lloyd of Think Graphic, not only for designing the lay out of the book, but also for his patience and his readiness to offer advice at all times.

Acknowledgement must also be made of the helpful assistance received from staff at Warwick County Record Office, Stratford-upon-Avon Library, The Shakespeare Birthplace Trust, Evesham Library and Bidford-on-Avon Library. Lesley Kirkwood, former Senior Local Studies Librarian at Warwickshire County Council, and her colleagues gave valuable advice about the management of the project, and Christina Evans, until recently Archaeological Project Manager with Warwickshire County Council's Museum Services and leader of the 'Buried under Bidford' project in 2007, has been a source of practical help and encouragement since the project's inception.

Most of all, the research team wishes to thank those Bidfordians who responded to the invitation to be interviewed and agreed to have their memories of village life recorded. Without their involvement, 'Yesterday's Children' could not have been written.

LIST OF ILLUSTRATIONS

Chapter Three: Earning a Living

Sheep washing, early twentieth century (Rodney Crompton Collection)
Arthur Stillgoe, an employee of the farmer Harry Smith (Rodney Crompton Collection)
Alan and Jack Mumford loading fruit (Hazel Mumford Collection)
Paddocks' lorry (Mike Paddock Collection)
Coventry Produce Market (CMHC, 1946)
E V Horseman, Elmfields Dairy (CMHC, 1946)
Broom Mill in the 1980s (Margaret Nilsson Collection)
Broom Mill, early twentieth century (Copyright, WCC, PH21/59)
Atkins and Thomas Ltd, Millers (Bidford Improvement Association (BIA), 1932
G H and E J Langston, Fruit and Vegetable Merchants (CMHC, 1946)
Langston's home-grown asparagus (Barry Langston Collection)
Pea-picking at Broom (Copyright, WCC, PH350/250)
Sill Brothers, Grocers, Corn and Provision Merchants (Shirley Collins Collection)
Shopping at Home (CMHC, 1946)
The Co-op (BIA, 1928)
Gray and Friend's Drapery Store (BIA, 1932)
Winnett's Butchers (Rodney Crompton Collection)
Winnett's Butchers (BIA, 1928)
Reliance Bus Company Staff (Rodney Crompton Collection)
Reliance Bus (Rodney Crompton Collection)
The Stratford Blue (BIA, 1932)

Chapter Four: Childhood

River Avon and bridge (Rodney Crompton Collection)
Infants School, 1931 (Frank Spiers Collection)
Junior School, 1914 (Copyright, WCC, PH352/30/93)
Florence Grove's School, 1927 (Dorothy Johnson Collection)
Bidford High School (Brian Cobb Collection)

Chapter Five: Time Off

'Going to Bidford', 1906 (Rodney Crompton Collection)
The Pleasure Boat Inn (Rodney Crompton Collection)
The Holly Bush (CMHC, 1946)
'Back again in Bidford' (Rodney Crompton Collection)
'OK Cocky' (Rodney Crompton Collection)
Bridge and charabanc, 1916 (Rodney Crompton Collection)
Boating on the River Avon (Rodney Crompton Collection)
Holland's Pavilion (Audrie Spiers Collection)
Holland's day-old chicks (CMHC, 1946)
Bidford Sports (Rodney Crompton Collection)
Horse Races and Sports Carnival Programme (BIA, 1928)
Carnival time in the 1950s (Copyright, Evesham Journal)
The Paddock family float, 1970s (Photograph courtesy of The Alcester Chronicle)
Methodist Chapel, 1981 (Jo Sawtell Collection)

Every effort has been made to trace copyright ownership of the illustrations included in the book. In some cases copyright has lapsed, in others investigations have been inconclusive. The owners of the collections referred to have all granted permission for their photographs and postcards to be used.

Church and its environs, late 1960s (By kind permission of Brewin Books)

INTRODUCTION

On 2 February 1901, the nation mourned the passing of an age, as Queen Victoria was laid to rest. The 'Evesham Journal' captured the mood in Bidford:

Here was observed a day of mourning, business being suspended, shops closed and blinds lowered. A muffled peal was rung at noon on the church bells and each morning since the death of Her Majesty the minute bell has been tolled. At two o'clock a large and thoroughly representative congregation assembled in the parish church...The solemn service commenced...by the rendering of Beethoven's Funeral March upon the organ at which Miss Fosbrooke officiated...In place of a sermon the Vicar briefly, but in the most appropriate terms, addressed the congregation... At the conclusion of the prayer, the hymn, 'Now the Labourer's task is O'er' was sung and the solemn strains of the Dead March from 'Saul' fittingly closed this memorial service.

The people of Bidford could have had little conception that day of the changes that were to affect the village during the new century. This book does not claim to be a history of twentieth century Bidford. Rather, it offers perspectives on village life based principally on the memories of 20 Bidfordians, recorded in interviews conducted by members of Bidford and District History Society. Interviewees were recommended via networks of personal contacts in the Bidford area. Their evidence mainly covers the five decades from the 1920s to the 1960s before the landscape of Bidford and the character of the village were transformed by the building of the relief road which was opened in 1979.

Most of Bidford's inhabitants today do not remember the village before the bypass. One of the main purposes of the book therefore is to open a window on to a largely forgotten world where agriculture remained the dominant means of employment and the High Street was the vibrant heart of a largely self-contained community with a strong sense of identity.

In addition to oral testimony, 'Yesterday's Children' draws on three written personal accounts: Barbara Comyns' autobiographical novel, 'Sisters by a River', published in 1947, an at once humorous and dark evocation of her childhood spent in Bidford between 1909 and 1926; Peggy Griffiths' colourful recollections, 'Sixty Glorious Years in Bidford' commencing in 1932; and Dr Michael Murray's entertaining manuscript memoirs of his life as a Bidford GP from 1928. Another rich vein of primary evidence is to be found in the weekly publication 'The Evesham Journal', whose pages provide by far the most extensive newspaper coverage of Bidford during the period. The National Census of 1901 has proved invaluable in determining patterns of employment, household structure and birthplace at the beginning of the century. Published every four years or so between 1900 and 1940, Kelly's Trade Directories contain incomplete lists of local businesses and trades, but can be useful in plotting changes in occupational patterns over the four decades. However, it is incidental details of postal collections, telephone numbers and school attendances, for example, that make the Directories such a fascinating and informative source.

Bidford Parish Magazine, the Minutes of the Parish Council, and School records, especially Log Books, which date back to the early years of the century, have all been extensively researched. If the Parish Magazines in the first half of the century were primarily used as a vehicle for the Vicar to exhort his parishioners on the importance of church attendance, they also provide an insight into many aspects of village life. The annual Carnival, Coronation and Jubilee celebrations and the impact of war on the people of Bidford are vividly documented. Parish Council Minutes would not be most people's choice for an entertaining read, but in Bidford they provide revealing glimpses of the issues that occupied the minds of Councillors and their constituents: for example, in 1956, the erection of public conveniences on the Big Meadow, and the 'vile smell' emanating from the still water that collected on the village bank after the river had been dredged. During the 1960s, discussions about the construction of a relief road appear with increasing regularity.

Additionally, a questionnaire was drawn up to elicit views on Bidford High School and especially reactions to its closure in 1985. Over 20 former pupils who attended the school during the seventies and eighties responded.

This body of primary evidence and the numerous secondary sources consulted provide the context for the oral reminiscences of 'yesterday's children'. Memory can be notoriously unreliable, especially among the elderly, but studies have shown that memories of childhood and early adulthood retain a much greater clarity and accuracy than memories of an individual's more recent past. This finding is amply borne out in the testimonies of the Bidford interviewees who were all able to provide detailed recollections of their childhood and schooldays, their early work experiences and special events. For many, the war years especially were indelibly etched in their memory.

When initially approached, a few interviewees felt they had little to relate; Ivy Webb, for example, claimed 'there's very little I can remember about me younger days'. However, prompts from the interviewer gradually unlocked her memory and produced the comment: 'Oh…it's just come to me'. Three-quarters of an hour later, after explaining how she helped her father to make rug mats, and regaling the interviewer with memories of her schooldays, her first date with her future husband, her work on the land and as a signal box operator at Broom during the war, the interview was concluded.

As with Peggy Griffiths in 'Sixty Glorious Years in Bidford', several interviewees are occasionally prone to 'good old days' nostalgia. However, the dominant tone in all oral testimonies, whether openly stated or implied, is unsentimental. For many, growing up in the thirties and forties, life was hard and lacking the material comforts that are taken for granted today. Betty Harris' reminiscences are very much in this vein, although 'if you try telling children, especially the grandchildren, about what we did in "the olden days", they think it's wonderful'.

The memories that inform this book, taken together, represent only a small part of the experiences of Bidford people during the last century. Other Bidfordians will have their own memories of village life, some complementary, others doubtless contradictory. Like all memories, those of the interviewees are not infallible. Wherever possible, the details in their accounts have been checked for accuracy with other testimony and by reference to primary and secondary evidence. Even the attitudes they display, as memory studies demonstrate, cannot always be assumed to have been the attitudes they held at the time they are recalling.

Oral evidence, like every other historical source, has its imperfections. The oral testimonies that have shaped this book, however, possess an intrinsic value as uniquely personal recollections of life in the riverside village of Bidford-on-Avon before it was transformed by the building of the bypass. As such they deserve to be heard.

Yesterday's Children

Molly Carter

Born in 1927 at Rock near Kidderminster where her mother ran a pub. Brought up by her mother's sister, Mrs Holtom, who lived in Bidford. Spent all her life in the village. Married to Bill Carter for 50 years before her death in July 2011.

Rodney Crompton

Born in 1935 in Evesham. Son of George Crompton, owner of the Reliance Garage on the Evesham Road and the Reliance Bus Company. Went to Bidford Infant and Junior School and then Alcester Grammar. Spent two years completing military service before returning to Bidford. Took over his father's business. Still living in the village.

Betty Harris

Born in Bidford in 1937 at home on Tower Hill where she lived until age 19. Daughter of Cyril Smith who worked for Alcester Builders and was also in the Royal Observer Corps in Bidford during World War II. Attended the village Infant and Junior Schools before going on to Bidford High School. Left the village when she married Leslie Harris and now lives in Stratford.

Charlie Haywood

Born in Bidford in 1929. Attended the village Infant and Junior Schools and then Alcester Grammar School. Worked as a fitter/engineer at Maudslay's in Great Alne until his retirement. Lifelong Bidford resident until his death in June 2012.

Norah Hiatt

Born in 1923 in Bidford. Lived on Tower Hill and attended the village Infant and Junior Schools. Went into domestic service after leaving school and subsequently married Thomas Hiatt from Bickmarsh. Had a son and daughter and was a lifelong Bidford resident. Died in September 2011.

Dorothy Johnson

Born in Bidford in 1922. Daughter of Edward Horseman MC who started a local dairy business. Lived in George's Elm Lane (originally Quarry Lane) and was brought up in the village. Left to train as a teacher and returned to Bidford to teach in 1954. Headmistress of Bidford Infant School from 1964 until her retirement in 1980. Still living in the village.

Mike Paddock

Born in 1933 in Bidford. Attended the village Infant and Junior Schools and then Alcester Grammar. Worked for his father, William Paddock on the family-owned Steppes Piece Farm, growing fruit and vegetables, then running it with his brother from 1960 until his retirement. Still living in the village.

Leslie Smith

Born in Bidford in 1920 and brought up in the village. In the territorial army in the 1930s and called up for regular service in 1938, leaving the army in 1946. Married Doris Hutchins from Essex in 1945 and moved back to Bidford working as a self-employed builder. Both he and his wife still living in the village.

Frank Spiers MBE

Born in 1925 at the Bull's Head pub. Son of the pub owners, Alfred and Victoria Spiers. Went to the Infant and Junior Schools, first Head Boy of Bidford High School. Employed for most of his working life at the Austin Motor Co in Longbridge. Parish Councillor since 1970, serving as chairman three times. In 1995 awarded the MBE for services to Bidford. Still living in the village.

Peter Warwick

Born in 1941. Moved to Bidford in 1947 when his father started a timber yard to add to the two he ran in Birmingham. After school in Stratford went to college in Redditch and then worked as a cabinet maker before working for his father. Married in 1962 and for the past thirty years has run the Harbour Guesthouse on the Salford Road.

Ivy Webb

Born in Marlcliff in 1926. One of five children to parents who were agricultural workers. Went to school in Bidford. Left school aged eleven, went into domestic service in Cleeve Prior, then into a factory in Alcester and during the war worked in the signal box at Broom Station. Last employment as lollipop lady at Bidford High School where her husband Frank was caretaker. Now lives in retirement in Bidford.

Thanks are also due to the following for additional information supplied, orally or in writing, as part of the research for this book: Shelford Bidwell, Bill Carter, Brian Cobb, Wendy Hemming, Mollie Henderson, Dinah Holder, Marjorie Kidson, Bet and Hedley Langston, Barbara Mumford, Shelagh Murray, Mary Paddock, Don Penn, Jo Sawtell, Gerhard Schober, Doris Smith and Pam Warwick.

Chapter 1

THE VILLAGE

A Community with Ambition

Piping Pebworth, Dancing Marston,
Haunted Hilborough, Hungry Grafton,
Dodging Exhall, Papist Wixford.
Beggarly Broom and Drunken Bidford.

Bidford as a settlement has a very long history, dating back at least to Roman times. Situated in a valley between two low hills and located on the northern bank of the principal river in the area, it is well placed as a river crossing point. At the intersection of the old Roman Icknield Street and the main east-west road between Stratford-upon-Avon and Evesham, it has historically been a focal point for local trade. In mediaeval times it was at the heart of the salt trade between Droitwich and the south, and on one of the drovers' routes, bringing animals from Wales and the west to central and south-east England.

The most colourful legend attaching to the village is the story of Shakespeare's visit for a drinking competition, where the best of Stratford's men took on the Bidford reserve team – and lost. The legend tells that Shakespeare composed a little rhyme for the winners, famously coining the term 'Drunken Bidford'. It is coupled with the story that he was unable to get back to Stratford, and spent the night sleeping off the evening's work under a crabapple tree just outside the village, returning home the following day, which some say was his birthday.

It is probable that Bidford was well known to him, since his brother-in-law lived at Bidford Grange, and the country girls' song in 'The Winter's Tale': 'Or thou goest to the Grange or Mill / If to either, thou dost ill' is reputedly a reference to family visits there.

As a settlement, Bidford's Saxon past was confirmed in 1921, when an eighth century burial ground was discovered close to the centre of the village and excavated over the following three years, yielding Saxon jewellery and weapons as well as the remains of those buried there. In 2010, Warwickshire Museum's Historic Environment Record decided to include Bidford in its ongoing Historic Towns project (set up in partnership with English Heritage), aimed at providing local historians with a research archive to assist them in the study of their local communities.

Bidford was in royal possession during the time of Edward the Confessor, and again during the reign of King John, who bequeathed it to his son-in-law. The fortunes of the village ebbed and flowed over the years, and neighboured as it was by the abbeys of Evesham and Alcester, as well as the business centre of Stratford-upon-Avon, it was very often obliged to play a secondary role in public life by comparison with its neighbours. Having been advanced in communications terms by the fifteenth century construction of its River Avon bridge, Bidford was a substantial place, but, compared with its neighbours, a minor township nonetheless.

The Parish of Bidford is therefore an ancient political entity, based on the village itself and the three adjacent settlements of Broom, to the north-west, and Marlcliff and Barton, south of the River Avon. At one stage there were four manors in the parish, and both Bidford Grange and Broom Hall remain as a reminder of former days. The parish traditionally made its living by agriculture and by riverside and country crafts. The power of the rivers (the confluence of the Arrow with the Avon lies on the south-western border of the parish) was used until recently for flour milling at Broom and (until the late nineteenth century) at Bidford Grange. Life in the parish has been

Bidford bridge, floods 1912 © Warwickshire County Council PH350/230

influenced in another significant way by the rivers, in the persistent flooding of low-lying areas after heavy rains or the thaw following a hard winter.

Broom Junction c1936-1939 © Roger Carpenter, Lens of Sutton Association

For almost three-quarters of a century the local railway network played a major role in Bidford's commercial and social life. Broom Junction Station was built as an exchange platform on the Barnt Green to Ashchurch line when the Stratford-upon-Avon and Midland Junction Railway opened in 1879. Providing easy access for passenger and freight traffic to Evesham, the West Country, Birmingham and beyond, it was always busier than Bidford's own station which was opened six years later on the Stratford-on-Avon and Midland line. Situated at the northern boundary of the village, it was inconvenient for most villagers and was largely used for the movement of market garden produce, bricks and domestic coal which passed through its small goods yard. As a result of falling demand in the post-war period passenger services were terminated at Bidford in 1947 and at Broom two years later, though freight traffic continued until 1962.

The trio of smaller units in the parish are separate, but remain an integral part of the parish of Bidford. Barton and Marlcliff both straddle the road from Welford-on-Avon to Cleeve Prior, the first village in Worcestershire. Each is centred upon a double bend in the road, with Barton hugging the river. At the dawn of the twentieth century Barton was described in the local trade directory as 'a small hamlet and village, consisting of a few scattered houses and a good inn'

Barton, looking towards The Cottage of Content
© Warwickshire County Council PH351/22

Larger and more complex than its neighbour, Marlcliff sits beneath the escarpment to which it owes its name, stretching for some distance along the four roads that create the double bend. The hamlet proper is down the hill (The Bank) leading towards the river. The centre lies around the 'village green' at the foot of the Bank where the road diverges into the built area on the right, and towards the Avon and the lock on the left.

Broom stands on three parallel roads: the High Street running east-west, with Mill Lane to its north and King's Lane to the south. A 1901 trade directory described Broom as 'a hamlet, but formerly a large village… a large water and steam flour mill… pleasantly situated south of Alcester… the seat of the Broom, Clarke and other families'. At the time, it had two pubs, the Broom Inn and the Holly Bush, both in the High Street. The present pubs have no shared heritage with their predecessors.

The places of interest in twentieth century Broom included the mill, which continued in business until 1988. It was demolished in 1995. The former Chapel of Ease is still in Mill Lane, but is now a private house. The railway station at Broom Junction no longer exists, though some of the structure may be seen between the River Arrow and the footpath to the west of it. Part of the western signal box is visible alongside the southbound carriageway of the A46, midway between the Bidford (B439) and Alcester (A435) junctions.

Much has been written regarding the historic ups and downs experienced by the village and its people through the centuries. Recent studies by Dr Richard Churchley and Professor Christopher Dyer have examined the fluctuations in their fortunes and reached the conclusion that Bidford has always been a community with ambition, but has never quite achieved greatness, largely on account of its geographical proximity to towns which, since Roman times, have had garrisons, and later, abbeys and charters to assert their own superiority. This was certainly the case during the twentieth century.

Aerial photograph of Bidford, 27 August 1946
© English Heritage, RAF Photography

Bidford in 2012
© Bidford and District History Society

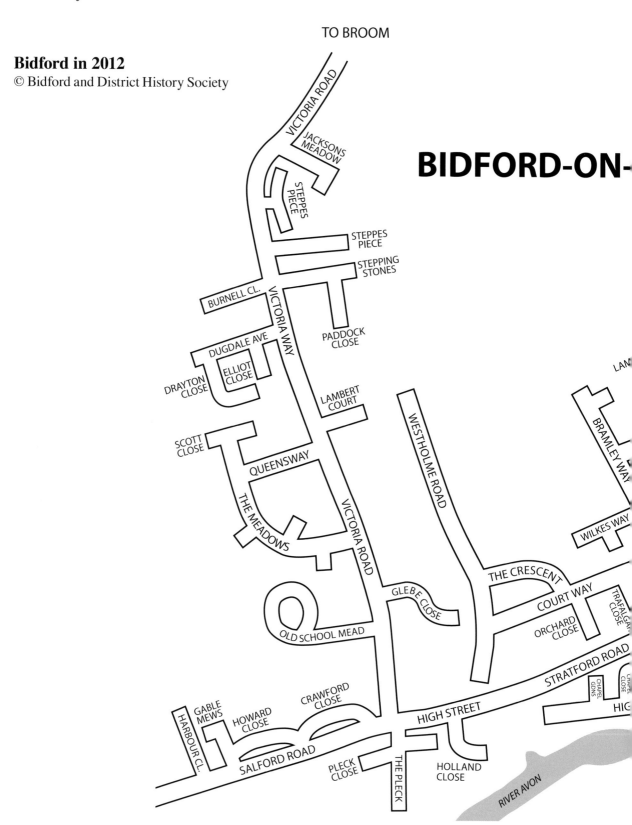

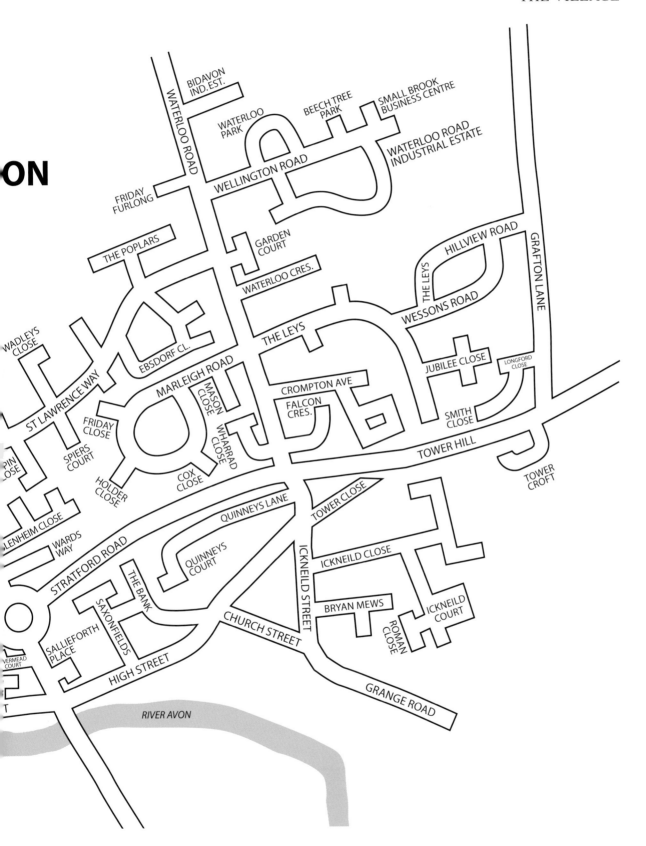

THE VILLAGE IN 1939

Using a combination of oral evidence, personal accounts, trade directories, advertisements and aerial photographs, it has been possible to reconstruct the main features in the village landscape at the outbreak of war in 1939, in particular the road network and the use and occupancy of buildings. A reconstruction of the village 40 years before the completion of the relief road provides a fixed point for contrasting the Bidford of 'Yesterday's Children' with the village as it is today.

Tower Hill to the Village Centre

Entering Bidford from the Stratford direction, visitors in 1939 would pass Grafton Lane on the right where the only hint of future residential development was a small row of 1920s council houses on the right hand side of the lane. Opposite Grafton Lane at the top of Tower Hill lay the path (Middle Lane) that led to the Observer Post set up in 1938 as preparations for war gathered pace. Descending the hill on the left hand side, visitors would pass the home of George Boshier, the architect, and 'Nurse' Boshier, the local midwife. Further down stood the large house of the wealthy farmer William Longford, whose fields stretched down to the Avon. Opposite the Plough Inn lived the painter, decorator and sign writer, Percy Bryan. Then came a little row of about three houses before the 'Ryck' yard, where Frank Spiers' uncle Fred Holder, a market gardener, kept his cattle. At the bottom of Tower Hill, on the corner of Icknield Street, stood the imposing Icknield House, which had been Fred Holder's home before he built Marleigh House on the left of Waterloo Road [1] in the mid-thirties.

On the opposite side of Tower Hill visitors would pass a line of houses, the last of which before the Plough Inn was the birthplace in 1924 of Norah Hiatt, one of a family of eight girls and two boys. At the foot of Tower Hill (the junction with Waterloo Road) lived the builder Charles Locke and his wife Martha, who kept a shop selling greengrocery and tobacco. According to Peggy Griffiths, the sisters Eleanor and Marjorie Porter, who were related to the Fosbroke family, 'lived in the beautiful black and white house on the corner of the High Street and Waterloo Road'. Marjorie Kidson remembers peering over the window sills at the dolls and other toys the sisters placed in the window. Until his death in 1925 the large neighbouring house had belonged to George Haynes Fosbroke, the Medical Officer of Health for Worcestershire, whose chauffeur, Bill Burford, lived next door. Two houses further down the High Street lived

[1] The site of the present-day Wharrad Close.

the coal merchant, Ray Cowper. As a boy Frank Spiers remembers delivering the coal with him on the horse and cart, riding Tommy the horse back to his field and then returning home on the handlebars of Mr Cowper's bicycle.

Charles Dowdeswell the saddler lived next door, and after him was a grocer's shop [2] belonging to Jackie and Ellen Froud 'You'd go there if you wanted a pack of biscuits or a tin of tomatoes', Frank recalled. The visitor's eye would next be drawn to the neighbouring house 'Avonbury', which in the 1920s had been the home of the old village doctor, Charles Hobbes. It had also been the site of the cockpit where cockfighting used to take place before it was made illegal during the nineteenth century. Remains of the cockpit are still visible underneath the floorboards.

Then came Bloodworth's the bakery firm. Two doors further down was a ladies' clothes shop which had formerly been the home of Mrs Warmington, who made teas and cakes for fishermen from Birmingham as they waited for the bus to take them home. Maud Seymour, a World War I widow, lived in the next house before the Post Office, at the point where the High Street widened to form the centre of the village.

Only two buildings fronted the High Street on the opposite side of the road between Icknield Street and Church Street. The first of these was the police house with cell attached, which was occupied in 1939 by PC Bill Munday. A garden area separated the police house from the old Falcon buildings on the corner with Church Street. These comprised five distinct dwellings, the first of which, an overhanging Elizabethan structure later pulled down to relieve traffic congestion, was Henrietta Houghton's greengrocers. Other 'Falcon' residents included Alf Bennett, who sold Sunday newspapers, and Tom and Maggie Zikking with their family of nine children.

The Falcon [3] is the most iconic building in Bidford. As venue for the drinking competition, it is part of the Shakespeare legend and allegedly the place where the

[2] Now Crown House, the home of Jane and Rodney Crompton.

[3] The Falcon is now divided into two private houses.

future Charles II addressed the Royalist troops in 1651 before marching them to the Battle of Worcester. It is also claimed that it was the use of the Falcon as a home for destitutes in the nineteenth century that led Lord Tennyson to write: 'The workhouse stands where was an inn'.

The Falcon © Warwickshire County Council, PH(n) 600/137/9 and 137/7

Village Centre to Marriage Hill

Beyond the wall bordering St Laurence Parish Church and churchyard stood King George House [4], the home of Arthur 'Yampy' Tedd's mother. Beyond the drive leading to the vicarage where the Rev Albert Harrison resided, was the Fisherman's Rest public house. Albert Gould held the licence in 1939, but for many years previously the pub had been under the management of Bill and Minnie Gardner. Arthur Tedd's sweetshop [5] was next door. Dorothy Johnson remembers there were no free samples: 'If you went in for toffee, he got a toffee hammer and used to measure it out. If it was overweight, he used to knock a bit off the toffee'. Then in succession came the Bidford on Avon Gas Co showroom, two cottages [6], Bill Kendall's boot and shoe shop and the house of the hairdresser Maurice Churchley. After the hairdresser's, Frank Spiers recalls, 'came a gap which we called Hemmings Lane down to the river' [7].

[4] Now the Estate Agent's Office.

[5] Now Bidford Pharmacy.

[6] Part of Bidford Health Centre stands where the two cottages used to be.

[7] When the river was dredged in the 1980s, the site of a Roman causeway was discovered at the end of Hemmings Lane.

Down Hemmings Lane was George Cope's dairy and then next in the High Street Annie Elsmore's grocers where Frank used to buy gobstoppers. Next door, John Davis' bakery, he remembers, 'made lovely lardy cakes, and the bread was delivered by hand …in a sort of push cart'. The bakery stood next to Olive Smith's shop which she divided between greengrocery and the exotic-sounding 'Oriental Café'. In former years the premises had housed 'Tinker' Wilcox's iron-monger's shop which Peggy Griffiths described as 'the Black Hole of Calcutta'. In 1939 the next two properties were private houses, but only a few years earlier the second of these, notable for its large front window, had been the ladies and gents' outfitters, Gray and Friend, run by Mr and Mrs Friend and their daughter Phyllis, who lived next door in the house they named 'Le Cove'.

Charles and Roland Hunt's butcher's shop would not have gone unnoticed by passing visitors if only for the smells emanating from the slaughterhouse. One of Frank Spiers' boyhood memories was of peeping in and seeing 'the poor cows and sheep'. The metal rail where they hung carcasses dressed for sale can still be seen. The last retail outlet before the White Lion Hotel and the bridge was Mrs Page's confectionery shop. 'A nice hotel' was Frank's verdict on the White Lion. 'People used to come down for a meal from Redditch and those parts, and then they'd come back up to the Bull to have a drink'.

In the centre of the village opposite the church stood the Post Office, which was managed by Jack and Peggy Griffiths. Peggy began a new line in beauty cosmetics such as face powder, vanishing cream and 'almost

The Bull's Head family
(Audrie Spiers Collection)

immoral' lipsticks and eye-shadow. An integral part of the Post Office, but entered by a separate door, was a drug store to which all medicines were sent down from the surgery in Victoria Road. Next to the Post Office was The Bull's Head, birthplace of Frank Spiers, where his widowed mother Victoria was the licensee.

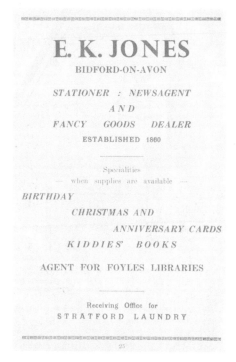

E. K. JONES
BIDFORD-ON-AVON

STATIONER : NEWSAGENT
AND
FANCY GOODS DEALER

ESTABLISHED 1860

Specialities
— when supplies are available —

BIRTHDAY
CHRISTMAS AND
ANNIVERSARY CARDS
KIDDIES' BOOKS

AGENT FOR FOYLES LIBRARIES

Receiving Office for
STRATFORD LAUNDRY

25

The Co-op emblem
(Sandra Parker Collection)

Then in turn came the house of Mr and Mrs Parker who owned Noakes and Croft, the building and decorating firm of George Langston and Sons, Lloyds Bank, the house where Marjorie Swift lived with her parents, and Jones' newsagents [8]. Frank remembers being paid five shillings (25p) a week for delivering the newspapers to Victoria Road and Broom, and Peggy Griffiths recalled how Mr Jones used to cycle 'every evening to Broom Junction to pick up the Evening Mail'. By 1939 his daughter Kathleen had taken over the running of the shop. Nearby stood the War Memorial, erected in 1923 to commemorate the Bidford men who gave their lives in the 1914-18 war.

Another landmark in the centre of the village in 1939 was the petrol pump that stood outside the large house of garage owner Gilbert Boshier, a little way down from The Bank. Shortly beyond where the High Street narrowed [9], stood the Jubilee, or Co-op Hall, a wooden building used regularly for dances and other forms of entertainment. Next door to it, on two floors, was the Bidford and Mickleton Co-op, and the observant visitor would notice the Co-op emblem, a 'Beehive', at the apex of the building, which may still be seen today. The upstairs housed offices and haberdashery, whilst clothes, grocery and a butcher's department occupied the ground floor.

[8] The present day site of Lloyds TSB Bank.
[9] Where the access to Saxonfields is today.

Mrs Emily Houghton's greengrocery shop nestled alongside the Co-op, and next to her was the wireless engineer Dick Mason who kept a large store of wireless accumulators and batteries. After three more cottages came the Mason's Arms [10], where the British Legion held their meetings in the club room at the back. Opposite the bridge was the shop of hairdresser 'Barber' Bennett and his wife, which sold all kinds of cottons, wools, postcards and buttons [11]. Next door to Bennett's emporium was the up-market grocers, Noakes and Croft [12]. 'They were the upper crust', in Frank Spiers' judgement: 'I mean, where we had Camp Coffee, they had proper coffee there'.

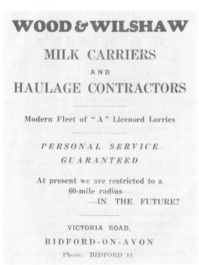

Miss Boshier's stylish ladies' dress shop was adjacent to Noakes and Croft. Next door was Florence Grove's private school, which Dorothy Johnson and her sister had attended some years earlier. Further along the High Street was Alex Whiting's fishmongers with a fish and chip shop attached that Norah Hiatt claimed 'looked like a prefab'. Whiting's was the first in a little chain of shops comprising Mrs Bullock's newsagents and toy shop and (immediately before Chapel Alley), Fred Prickett's butchers, which like Hunt's, also had a slaughterhouse on the premises.

Beyond Chapel Alley, so-named after the original nineteenth century Wesleyan Methodist chapel which stood at the top of the rise, Frank Spiers' aunt and uncle, Charlie and Maud Vincent, had their fruit and vegetable shop opposite Bell Court. Frank remembers how 'Auntie Maud used to go round to all the farms and buy antiques. The antiques really did well'. A row of houses brought visitors to Westholme Road, which at the time comprised no more than eight houses. At the far end was Wood and Wilshaw's transport business, which collected milk from local farms. According to Rodney Crompton, the rattling of empty milk churns along the unmade road at 4.00am served as an effective, if unwelcome, alarm clock.

[10] Now The New Saxon.
[11] This building was demolished to make the short access road between the bridge and the B439 roundabout.
[12] The present One-Stop.

After Westholme Road was the 'Reliance Garage', owned by Rodney's father George Crompton, for several years Chairman of Alcester Rural District Council. The garage had moved from its original site across the road in 1935 [13]. The junction with Victoria Road was the point where the High Street became Salford Road. On the corner of Victoria Road and Salford Road was Alice Drew's sweetshop, which did a good trade from the children going to school in Victoria Road. Thereafter, the main road was lined by orchards and houses until the village boundary, which was marked by the Lieutenant Round memorial bench at the foot of Marriage Hill, dedicated by his wife at the end of the 1914-18 war, and still in position today.

High Street, the tall building with a canopy on the right hand side is the Assembly Rooms
© The Francis Frith Collection

On the southern side of the High Street, after passing the mediaeval bridge, visitors would find their attention caught by the oppressive front of a two-storey building known as the Assembly Rooms[14] The ground level comprised a number of shops whose occupants in 1939 included Miss Mabel Wakefield, who sold fruit, vegetables and sweets, and Charles Broadley, a corn and flour merchant. The upper storey was used for dances and as the local cinema, but the Assembly Rooms were never as popular as the Jubilee Hall, because the latter, unlike the Assembly Rooms, was situated at ground floor level and consequently more accessible.

[13] Occupying the site which is now Budgens.
[14] The site of the Bridge Restaurant today.

Between the Assembly Rooms and the Pleasure Boat Inn stood a building used by Minnie Gardner to store the osiers collected from osier beds opposite the church, and a cottage lived in by her sister, Miss Rimell [15]. Minnie had a reputation for swearing and intimidating behaviour, whereas, according to Peggy Griffiths, Miss Rimell 'was so sweet and pious it was difficult to believe that they were related'.

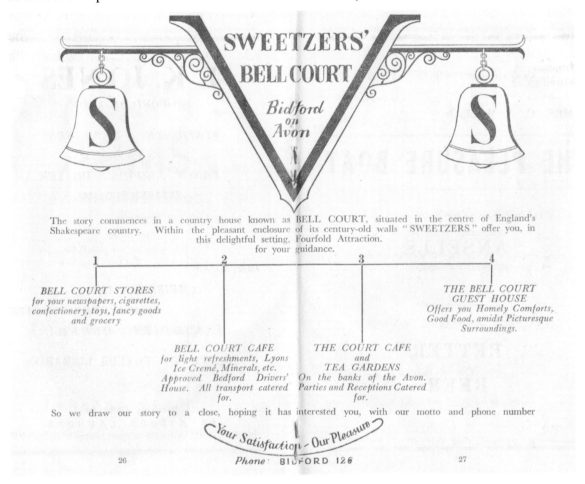

SWEETZERS'
BELL COURT

Bidford on Avon

The story commences in a country house known as BELL COURT, situated in the centre of England's Shakespeare country. Within the pleasant enclosure of its century-old walls "SWEETZERS" offer you, in this delightful setting, Fourfold Attraction. for your guidance.

1	2	3	4
BELL COURT STORES *for your newspapers, cigarettes, confectionery, toys, fancy goods and grocery*	**BELL COURT CAFE** *for light refreshments, Lyons Ice Cremé, Minerals, etc. Approved Bedford Drivers' House. All transport catered for.*	**THE COURT CAFE** *and* **TEA GARDENS** *On the banks of the Avon. Parties and Receptions Catered for.*	**THE BELL COURT GUEST HOUSE** *Offers you Homely Comforts, Good Food, amidst Picturesque Surroundings.*

So we draw our story to a close, hoping it has interested you, with our motto and phone number

Your Satisfaction – Our Pleasure

26   *Phone*: BIDFORD 126   27

Next door to the Pleasure Boat, Frank Spiers remembers, Mr and Mrs Sweetzer kept a shop that 'sold everything, especially toys' [16]. The Sweetzers lived in the adjoining Bell Court, where the novelist Barbara Comyns had been born thirty years earlier. Three or four houses down the road from Bell Court was Cicely Lea's sweetshop. She had taken it over from her mother Annie, who by 1939, having turned their home into a boarding house, also taught shorthand and typing. Her sister, Mona Hever, lived in the same house and gave piano lessons.

[15] The Pleasure Boat is now The Frog (formerly the Frog and Bulrush), and the buildings were in due course demolished to provide a car park for the pub.

[16] In recent years, it has been used as a wine merchant's, and more recently as a betting shop.

Rounding the bend at the bottom of the High Street towards Salford Road, visitors would come to Holland's Pleasure Gardens. 'Lovely, they were', muses Frank Spiers. 'All punts and rowing boats, and there was a little steamer to take you downstream to Cleeve Prior'. The next turning on the same side (The Pleck) led to the Gasworks. According to George Crompton, the manager used to sit on top of the small gasometer on Sundays to increase the gas pressure. Further along the main road, Moore Bros had their haulage business on the site of George Crompton's first garage. Two houses positioned well back from the road separated Moore Bros from Alf Foster the coal merchant, whose wife performed the important village role of laying out the dead. Facing visitors leaving the village was the steep incline of Marriage Hill, now much lowered. Just before reaching it, there were two rows of houses on the left hand side, at the foot of the hill. 'The Blocks', so-named because they were made from concrete, were the older of the two.

Charlie Haywood recalls that one of his friends was living at The Blocks in 1939. They offered very little in the way of amenity for residents, and were for a long time marked out for demolition, finally ordered by Alcester Rural District Council in 1959, once Crompton Avenue had been built and tenants could be rehoused there.

Around the Village

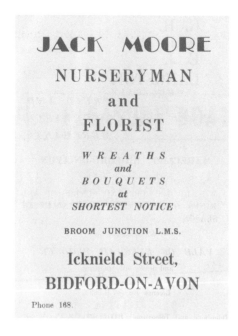

JACK MOORE

NURSERYMAN
and
FLORIST

WREATHS
and
BOUQUETS
at
SHORTEST NOTICE

BROOM JUNCTION L.M.S.

Icknield Street,
BIDFORD-ON-AVON

Phone 168.

If anyone passing through the village in 1939 had had the time to explore the roads leading away from the High Street, they would have discovered that apart from Icknield Street and neighbouring Church Street, building and commercial development was patchy. Entering Icknield Street from the High Street, they would see a line of mainly black and white cottages along the right hand side of the street. On the opposite side [17], Frank Spiers recalls, the market gardener Jack Moore 'had his greenhouses and grew super tomatoes and flowers'. The first houses on that side (Coronation Row) marked the coronation of Edward VII. Charlie Haywood was born there (at No 1) in 1929. One of the two other houses after Coronation Row was to become Frank Spiers' home after he got married.

[17] On land that is now Icknield Close.

Further down, Frank remembers, 'was George Bryan with his sons Bernard and Bill, who did building and plumbing, and were also wheelwrights. Bernard was a good signwriter as well. I can see him now painting gipsy caravans'. Next to the Bryans was the forge, where Harry Wilcox plied his blacksmith's craft. The circular iron plate he used for setting the rims on cartwheels can still be seen there. Then came the Fire Station, built in the mid-thirties to replace the old station by the Mason's Arms.

The Fire Brigade, 1936
© Evesham Journal
Back Row L to R:
H Wilkes, H Collins(Captain),
S Smith, H Bennett, J Smith,
C Manders
Front Row L to R: J Russell,
E Wilkes, G Smith,
F Butler, W Gardiner.

Moving round and into Grange Road lived Elijah Bryan, a carrier who in 1939 was still using a horse and cart. Alf Ash the butcher, who had formerly worked for Hunt's in the High Street, was also on the corner with Grange Road. A few private cottages made up the other buildings on that side of the road.

On the opposite side beyond the cottages was Avonside, the impressive surgery, dispensary and home of Dr Crawford until 1935, when he built Blythe House in the adjoining grounds. Next door but one lived Fred Houghton, the monumental stonemason, who had taken over the business from his former employer Mr Davis, a few years before. Between his house and the road was the Welfare Hut, where welfare payments were made and the Parish Council held its meetings. During the war it would be used as the centre for distributing ration books, weighing babies, and dispensing cod liver oil and orange juice to the very young.

Heading back towards the High Street, visitors would pass the cemetery, opened earlier in the decade. Between the cemetery and the churchyard was a narrow track leading down to the river, and known locally as 'Duffus Lane'. According to Rodney Crompton, all the children went swimming at 'Duffus' since the water was shallow all the way down to the bridge.

Edwin Skuse was an erector of stained glass windows, and lived in the house that is now the Dentist's surgery, facing the churchyard in Church Street. Frank Spiers' main memory of Mr Skuse and his wife, Minnie, was that 'they were always smartly dressed'. Next door lived 'Cloggy' Busby, manager of the local football team. The Infant School (now the Church Hall) came next, then a private house, followed by the Falcon building.

On the opposite side of the High Street, two roads connected Bidford with its neighbouring communities. Waterloo Road, which for much of the early twentieth century was known in the village as Alcester Lane, was thinly populated in 1939, especially on the western side. Most of the buildings on the eastward side were concentrated in a row of about ten houses some 300 yards north of the High Street. Among these, the largest and most striking was Waterloo House, the home of Tommy Luker. Another, nicknamed 'Home Guard House' according to Charlie Haywood, was to become the Bidford Home Guard HQ during the war. The only trading premises on Waterloo Road belonged to the Bidford Brick and Tile Company, and were strategically situated adjacent to Bidford railway station.

Broom Street, now Victoria Road © Warwickshire County Council PH350/201

Compared with Waterloo Road, Victoria Road in 1939 was more heavily developed and the roadside landscape more varied. Just a short distance from the High Street on the right stood two houses built in the early 1930s. The first of these, named 'Fairacres', belonged to George Crompton, the garage owner. The second, 'Green Gates', was the home of Dr Michael Murray, and also housed the surgery. Further up the hill was a bungalow, where Shelford Bidwell, the future owner of Bidford Boats, lived with his parents. Then came three pairs of semi-detached properties set back from the road and only completed in 1939.

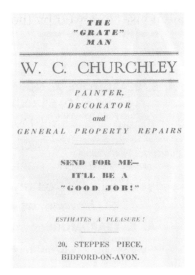

A line of older detached houses, including 'Glenfield', 'Sunnyside' and 'The Elms', dating from the first decade of the century, were situated a little further along. The gaps between them had been partially filled during the inter-war years by pairs of semi-detached properties. One of these was the home of Alfred Edge, the stationmaster at Broom Junction. In the same row lived Fred Coleman of the building firm Coleman and Tyas, Joseph Robbins the bootmaker, Laurence Bradley the blacksmith and Albert Smith, the oil merchant. Immediately before the right-hand bend was Steppes Piece, a planned development of about 30 council houses, built in 1932.

Visitors looking left along Victoria Road from Mrs Drew's corner shop would only see fields until their eye was caught by Bidford Primary School, built as a National School in 1872. The school stood here for 130 years until it moved to its present location in Bramley Way in 2002 [18]. Beyond the school was a compact line of houses dating from between 1900 and 1920, some of which were built as homes for the employees of the Bidford and Mickleton Co-op. Set in spacious grounds, Victoria House was the largest among these properties. A little way beyond Victoria House was the grocer's shop of George Trayford, who was ideally situated to attract the custom of children attending Bidford Senior School after it opened in 1938. The shop made its own ice cream, which ensured its popularity with school pupils. But it was lost to the village when new estates were built in the 1970s at The Meadows, Queensway and Scott Close.

Despite building development since the start of the century, particularly along Victoria Road, and to a lesser extent Waterloo Road and Grafton Lane, the village in 1939 bore little physical resemblance to modern day Bidford. Behind the line of houses on the western side of Victoria Road, as Frank Spiers recalls, 'there was no Dugdale Avenue or Burnell Close. It was all agricultural land and orchards'.

[18] The ageing school was replaced with a modern, purpose built Junior and Infant School closer to the population centre of the village. The site on which it had stood was developed as a housing area, named as Old School Mead. Some older buildings on the site were restored for housing, and named Warner Court, in memory of Arthur Warner, Headmaster from 1917 to 1946.

At the other end of the village between Grafton Lane and Waterloo Road, 'Wessons Road and Hill View Road, The Leys and Crompton Avenue were grazing fields for cattle and sheep, and orchards'. On the west side of Waterloo Road:

Marleigh Road and the Quinney's Lane area was agricultural land used for growing sprouts, cabbages, runner beans, potatoes etc. Saxonfields was the Co-op meadow where children played. St. Laurence Way, Bramley Way and The Poplars were orchards and smallholdings. Where the Junior School is was where Fred Wilkes had his milking cows.

Chapter 2

HOUSE AND HOME

High Street. © Warwickshire County Council (Francis Frith Collection) PH21/35

Home comforts

Photographs of Bidford in the first half of the twentieth century show a village of picturesque timber framed cottages and an interesting assortment of period styles along the High Street. Yet domestic life for many people was far from idyllic for much of the period, with houses lacking many of the basic amenities regarded today as essential.

There was no mains water in the village until 1932. Villagers either used the wells or they had water tanks into which the water had to be pumped. Pumping provided Frank Spiers with a source of pocket money:

> *Mr and Mrs Parker who owned Noakes and Crofts (the grocery shop) lived*
> *next to the Bull. One of my jobs when I was a boy was to go and pump*

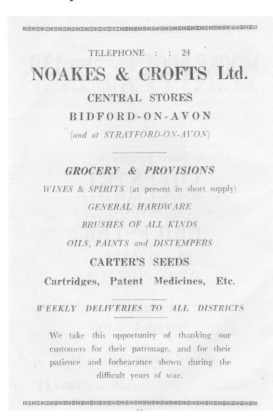

TELEPHONE : : 24

NOAKES & CROFTS Ltd.

CENTRAL STORES

BIDFORD-ON-AVON

(and at STRATFORD-ON-AVON)

GROCERY & PROVISIONS

WINES & SPIRITS (at present in short supply)

GENERAL HARDWARE

BRUSHES OF ALL KINDS

OILS, PAINTS and DISTEMPERS

CARTER'S SEEDS

Cartridges, Patent Medicines, Etc.

WEEKLY DELIVERIES TO ALL DISTRICTS

We take this opportunity of thanking our customers for their patronage, and for their patience and forbearance shown during the difficult years of war.

the water up into the cistern. I used to get half a crown a week for that, and Miss Bloxham… the housekeeper… always gave me a nice cake.

Before the Bull's Head was connected to the mains,

…all the water we had was from a pump in the pub passageway and water from the cistern under the kitchen for soft water …Water for washing and having a bath in a zinc bath was heated in the copper. We'd take it from the cistern using a bucket to fill the copper which was heated up by a fire underneath to do the washing. We had a bath once a week in a zinc bath in the kitchen on Saturday night at about 5.30 before the pub opened.

With the truck his father made him, Frank took stone jars of water to people who had run out of water when the well ran dry. Mr and Mrs Lloyd lived in a bungalow in Westholme Road and

> *…when they ran out of water I'd get my little truck and … take two big jars of water up to them on my way to school – they'd give me half a dozen biscuits for that!*

Houses in Salford Road, 1930s.
© Warwickshire County Council PH350/233

It was many years before all houses were connected to the mains. Most of the houses in Marlcliff still did not have running water by the time Peter Warwick moved there in 1962. They were lucky as they had a cold water tap in the kitchen but no waste drain, just a communal ditch. Betty Harris remembers that it was not until the late 1940s that running water and a toilet were installed in their house on Tower Hill:

> *We had a bath by the fire right through my teens until I left home. A lot of the cottages didn't have bathrooms. We were one of four cottages that shared a water pump outside.*

This must have deterred many from having regular baths. Dr Murray records the extreme case of 'a very scruffy, dirty and smelly individual' who came into his consulting room in 1934. The doctor was reluctant to examine him:

> *I very nearly sent him home for a bath first, only he did not seem very well and probably the shock of both would have made him worse… I asked him eventually when he had last had a bath and he replied, 'I don't rightly remember, Doctor, but I was once sponged over in Mesopotamia in 1916'.*

'Bucket and Chuck it'

Toilet facilities were even more primitive. In most cases toilets were situated at the bottom of the garden and were 'soil lavatories' with no sewage system. Betty Harris dreaded using the toilet at night. She and her sister Pat were afraid of the dark:

> *It was a long way as a child going down the garden. I used to put my gloves on because I got cold. Pat used to laugh at me! [At first] we used to take a candle [and then] a lantern…after the war we got proper toilets with water but they were still outside so, if it was raining, you got wet!*

The customers' toilet at the Bull's Head, according to Frank Spiers, was 'a double one side by side and in holiday times it got quite full! It was down the bottom near the pigsty. There was no toilet paper, newspapers would be left in the toilets'.

Ivy Webb, who lived in Marlcliff, vividly remembers her long walk:
We weren't even just outside the back…there were seven houses and we had to walk

Marlcliff © Warwickshire County Council PH351/13

past six of them right the way down yards and yards to our little whatsit. It was in the coalshed. Mum…used to go down there last thing at night before going to bed, she used to get Dad to go down with her and stand outside the toilet.

Barbara Comyns, whose family was amongst the better off in Bidford, described how toilet facilities for the family at Bell Court early in the century were markedly superior to those of the servants:

The maids had their own toilet about a hundred yards from the house across the yard…it was built of brick and had rather a rotten door painted brown. [Inside the toilet was] just a rough piece of wood with a hole and bucket underneath… the maids never grumbled about their lavatory although we had some good ones with chains in the house.

The 'middy men' used to come round at night and empty the toilets. Barbara Comyns remembered how her sister Chloe would stay awake the night the 'middy man' came on his rounds. She said his cart had oil lamps hanging from it and smelt simply dreadful, and he would cry, 'Muck, muck, bring out your muck'.

West End of High Street Rodney Crompton Collection

Toilet facilities were little better when Rodney Crompton was growing up during the forties. At school, 'the toilets out the back were "bucket and chuck it", and down at the bottom of the High Street they were all "bucket and chuck it". As for 'chucking it',

A lorry with a big tank on the back of it came to collect it, often when we were coming back from school. You used to try and work out which way the wind was blowing and how long you could hold your breath while running! I could do an awful lot of running along there!

After 1850 the use of gas for street lighting and for lighting private homes steadily expanded and the introduction of the 'penny in the slot' pre-payment meter in 1889 enabled gas companies to extend supplies to homes lower down the social scale. A private Gas Company was established in Bidford in 1869 in what is now The Pleck. However, by the 1930s, when it was taken over by the Cheltenham Gas Company, not all the village was connected. According to Frank Spiers,

> We had gas lights only in the main street. There was gas lighting in the church too. [At the Bull's Head] we had gas lighting downstairs but not upstairs. We had candles upstairs. Think how dangerous it was with straw mattresses and candles for light!

The 1930s saw the advent of electricity to the village. It was many years however before some homes were connected. Betty Harris recalls:

> We were the only cottage on Tower Hill that ...had it. Some had it in the hall but didn't have it upstairs.

Frank Spiers had to have both mains water and electricity installed when he bought his first house in Icknield Street in 1953 and it was at least 1960 before Charlie Haywood's home had electricity. However, some like Betty Harris never lost their affection for the old oil lamps: 'they were lovely, a soft light, just a twinkle'.

Charlie Haywood as a boy in Icknield Street, 1935
Charlie Haywood Collection

The lack of home comforts was a feature of many dwellings. Ivy Webb recalled how:

> Dad could never afford carpets. Used to be lino and rugs then on the floor... Dad used to make the rug mats and we kiddies [in turn] had used to... have a peg to peg them... and we used to cut up the old rags and then help him to put them through.

Space was often at a premium. As a child Charlie Haywood knew of at least two families with ten children and only three bedrooms. In Ivy Webb's case:

45

We had two bedrooms. Mum and Dad had one of them with the youngest in a bed beside them and then us others would have to sleep in the other room...four girls and one boy all in the same bed!

Home service

Delivering the Bread. © Warwickshire County Council PH352/30/51

Until refrigerators became common during the second half of the century, the difficulty in storing food for a long period made regular shopping necessary. Bidford boasted a range of food shops and most shopping was done locally. Basic necessities like bread, milk and groceries were often delivered to people's homes. For a period in the 1930s, Dorothy Johnson's family had its bread delivered by Mr Elsmore:

> *My mother used to make all our cakes and stuff, but on Saturdays we were allowed to go to Mr Elsmore's van. He used to open the back and we could choose five cakes for sixpence...My mother used to say they were terrible; we used to think they were fantastic. They were those Viennese Whirls with a bit of jam. We used to think things like that were magic!*

Peggy Griffiths' milkman, George Cope, brought the milk by pony and trap in a large churn, 'which was bound by brass or copper and polished until it looked like gold'. In fact, almost everything used to come to the door, according to Dorothy Johnson:

> *A big van used to come around with all the paraffin and oil and matches, candles and stuff like that and then another van came round with Corona pop.*

Pig roast, 1911. Rodney Crompton Collection

Betty Harris, growing up in the forties, recalled:

> *Up the hill where we lived there was a girl who was an assistant at the Co-op and on a Monday she would come down and take the grocery order. Then they would deliver the next day.*

Rodney Crompton remembers that for many years Flowers brewery even delivered bottled beer to the door. There was a good selection of clothes shops in the High Street according to Betty Harris: 'We also bought materials as there were shops selling materials. There was a lady in Grafton Lane who made dresses for my sister and me. We were often dressed the same'. 'Looking back', wrote Peggy Griffiths,

> *... it seems we were well and truly catered for, and waited upon, and our custom was greatly valued. Now we have to serve ourselves and carry our purchases in plastic bags.*

Pigs and 'Plum Jerkum'

As well as patronising local shops, Bidford families engaged in various forms of self-sufficiency, most commonly the keeping of a pig and the production of home-made wine. Frank Spiers recalls that:

> *Dad always kept a pig at the top of the garden. Of course us children made*

a pet of the pig, we used to help feed him. Some of his feed was the hops and malt from the beer barrel - he always seemed to enjoy it. Once when Dad was ill, Grandad Allen came and helped me; we gave the pig too many slops out of the barrel and the pig fell over and he was grunting as though he was laughing! With help we got him back on his feet.

The pigs were always killed in the autumn. For much of the interwar period the 'official' pig killer was local taxi driver Ern Wilkes. It could be an upsetting experience for the children. When Dorothy Johnson's pig was killed, her father used to say to her mother, 'Take the girls into Stratford' to get them out of the way. Frank Spiers remembers:

When November came, it was time for [the pig] to be killed at the top of the yard at the Bull's Head…Us children – Dinah, Fred and myself – we were in the pub and we cried when we heard the pig squealing.

Whenever a pig was killed, according to Bill Carter, 'we shared it with the neighbours'. Nothing went to waste. The pig not only provided plenty of bacon and ham, Frank Spiers' Granny Allen also made brawn out of the pig's head and tail:

I would hold the chitterlings over the bath for Dad to clean them out with hot water. We often used the bath about half an hour after this!

Rodney Crompton remembers eating things like pig's trotters:

They were smashing, and brawn as well. We used to make soup with hock, it was so thick the spoon stood up in it!

Pig meat was the commonest but not the only source of home-produced food. Numerous families kept hens, and some families, like Dorothy Johnson's, turkeys also. Rabbits were another abundant food supply. Frank Spiers recalls:

They were caught in traps, we caught loads at the back of the Bull. They made a lovely stew and roast rabbit was good too. It made a nice change from pig meat and nice to have something that wasn't salted.

Apart from meat, villagers grew their own produce so most had a plentiful supply of fruit and vegetables in their gardens. Betty Harris explained:

We had a long garden so we grew a lot of vegetables. Everybody did really. We all had the front gardens up, you see.

One of the main uses for home-grown fruit and vegetables was in the production of home-made wine. It was common to be asked to step inside someone's house for a 'glass of home-made'. According to Rodney Crompton:

Everybody made it – plum, rhubarb, pea pod, potatoes. The Germans made schnaps out of it. We had oat schnaps, peach, raspberry – it all tasted the same, mind!

Frank Spiers' father and friends drinking 'home-made', c1930 Frank Spiers Collection

Frank Spiers' father

... made it in the shed just out the back. We used to pick dandelions, then there were cowslips, he made parsnip wine and plum wine which was always called 'plum jerkum', then there was home-made cider and elderflower. That was made in bottles unlike the other types which were made in barrels.

What Les Smith remembers in particular about the wine made by Frank's father and others was its strength. This was also a characteristic of the parsnip and dandelion wine made by Charlie Haywood's parents. Since each barrel contained up to 40 gallons of the home-made brew, the potential for 'drunken Bidford' certainly existed.

'In the family way'

Serious boy and girl relationships did not normally develop at an early age during the first half of the century. In 1942 when Frank Spiers 'walked out' with a girl, he was 17. Rodney Crompton, 10 years Frank's junior, echoed the predominant male view of the time: 'The last thing you wanted to do was talk about marriage at the age of 18'. More important was the need to make a living before settling down to married life. 'You could have a lot of friends who were girls', and such friendships 'were far less heavy'.

The parents of Frank and Rodney, like most parents, told them nothing about sex. A further inhibiting factor was the absence of any readily available contraception, which made young men like Frank 'frightened of putting anyone in the family way'. In practice however pre-marital pregnancies were common. A national survey in 1938-9 revealed that 30 percent of all women conceived their first child before marriage. In

Bidford, on those occasions when a young woman became pregnant the matter was kept very hush-hush. Most girls in this situation got married, 'rhubarb' weddings, as Charlie Haywood called them, because they were 'forced'. However,

If a girl disappeared from the village, you knew what had happened. Girls would go to a relative outside the village until the baby was born. Many babies must have been adopted.

Rodney Crompton remembers one particular tragedy when a girl committed suicide on realising she was pregnant.

The most vulnerable women were those who lived outside the protective cocoon of their own family environment. Barbara Comyns recalls:

Mammy was very easy-going with the maids, they had masses of time off, and could stay out as long as they liked, so they often had babies, and we never knew they were having them till they were almost due and the old doctor's wife would come and tell Mammy and the poor girl would have to go.

Illegitimacy proved quite lucrative for Bidford's medical practitioners in the thirties, as Dr Murray recounts:

Many women came down to the country to have their illegitimate babies and…we had two houses in the practice which catered exclusively for these types of girls. They were mainly of the wealthy classes and could afford everything of the best and in the main one got well paid for the services one carried out.

Illegitimate births rose during the Second World War. In Bidford, of the 1,762 confinements attended by Dr Murray and his partners over a four-year period, 962 (nearly 55%) were illegitimate. The wish to avoid war service was the reason given to Dr Murray by five girls who gave birth on three occasions, and by 70 girls who gave birth twice.

Illness and death

One of the most sought-after people in Bidford during the twenties and thirties was the midwife, Nurse Boshier, the wife of local architect George Boshier. In an age when doctors received little training in obstetrics and when most births still took place at home, Nurse Boshier, according to Frank Spiers, 'brought most of the babies into the world at that time'.

Although infant mortality fell from 142 per 1000 births in 1900 to 55 by 1938, whooping cough, measles, scarlet fever, pneumonia, diphtheria, tuberculosis and polio posed serious threats to a child's health. In the absence of antibiotics (penicillin was not available until 1941), some remedies were imaginative to say the least. Dorothy Johnson remembers having whooping cough, 'because that's when they were tarring the lane for the very first time'. Dr Murray said to Dorothy's mother: '"Go and stand by the tar machine and tell her to breathe in and out", so that's what I had to do while these men were working'.

Scarlet fever was more serious. Dorothy's sister had scarlet fever when she was about nine and

> *... was taken away in a horse and carriage at night because nobody had to know she'd got it because of the milk business and nobody was allowed to go and see her.*

She was taken to Alcester Fever Hospital as were those diagnosed with diphtheria or TB. According to Frank Spiers, people knew the significance of the arrival of an ambulance in the village: 'If the ambulance came, you kept away from it'.

Diphtheria and tuberculosis were quite common during the first quarter of the century, and there were several cases in Bidford during the thirties. The BCG vaccine to combat TB did not become available until after World War II, but immunisation against diphtheria became widespread during the 1930s and Frank recalls receiving the 'jab' in school. Polio remained a threat during this period. Frank's younger brother Fred had a mild attack. Fred 'was very poorly as a kid. He had double pneumonia a couple of times' and couldn't take part in sports. Impetigo, which brought sufferers out in pimples, was less serious but very contagious. Charlie Haywood remembers how he and some of his friends tried to catch it deliberately by rubbing their hands over an infected child's face in order to get two weeks off school.

Surgery was regarded as the most effective way of dealing with complaints which today would be treated by other means. For example, it was commonplace for children to have their tonsils removed. Frank Spiers had the operation in the old Stratford Hospital in 1932 when he was seven and was kept in for about a week: 'Gawd! I can see meself now, climbing off the stretcher on to the bed'.

Before the National Health Service was established in 1948, hospital treatment was not free for the majority of the population. Frank's family was one of many that paid about sixpence a week into the Stratford Hospital Fund. Moreover, doctors derived their income from the fees they charged their patients with the result that, as Dorothy Johnson explained, 'you didn't have the doctor unless it was necessary'. After the war, recalls Dr Murray,

> ...things got very tough for people living on fixed incomes...and I had quite a few patients who said ... they would not be able to pay in full at least, but as they were elderly, and I was much younger, would I be good enough to leave my accounts over or perhaps take half as a token amount to keep the account alive, and I could be paid later if things improved or after they were dead.

Dental treatment also had to be paid for. Owing to the sparse provision of dental care, tooth decay was widespread. Bidford was not served by a dentist until the 1930s, and then, in the person of Mr Widdowson from Birmingham, only once or twice a week. He rented a room from Ern Wilkes, the local pig killer, and Frank Spiers remembers going to him on a couple of occasions:

> If you knew you'd got to go to the dentist, you never had any sleep the night before! I'd be frightened to death.

Charlie Haywood's friends even referred to the dentist as 'the butcher' because he was so 'rough'.

Major dental operations required the presence of both dentist and doctor. Dorothy Johnson had her wisdom teeth out when she was about 14. She normally went to Mr Shovelton in Evesham and he and Dr Murray

> ... came to the house and it was done in my bedroom. Dr Murray said to Mr Shovelton, 'How many teeth?' He said, 'All four'. 'Oh God', Dr Murray said, 'I've only brought enough ether for two'.

Doctors were regarded as people of consequence in the village. When the century dawned, the resident doctor was Charles Edward Hobbes. By 1908 he had been joined by Henry Marston Crawford, who was referred to by Barbara Comyns as 'the handsome doctor'. 'A nice chap, Dr Crawford. Good for the village he was', was the view of Frank Spiers. Dr Michael Murray, who arrived in Bidford in 1928 as an assistant to Dr Crawford, recalls that six months before the latter's death in 1943, he 'went blind in one eye and then in the other eye a month later, but so strong was [his] courage and strength of character that he had...three months later conquered Braille'.

Dr Murray's own arrival in Bidford caused quite a stir. According to Dorothy Johnson, 'the village was agog when this gorgeous young doctor came'. People soon became aware of his lifelong passion for horse racing. Rodney Crompton recalls:

Dr Murray cutting a sod, 1950s © Stratford Herald
L to R: Bill Holder, Dr Murray, Nathan Locke, Gordon Richards, Dorothy Bateman, Bill Churchley

*You could guarantee that if you went to see him while the races were on,
you would be in and out of the surgery in 32 seconds! On his chair he had
the binoculars with all the race tags on. If you saw those, you knew you
wouldn't be very long.*

The esteem with which these two doctors were held was illustrated by the reaction
to their weddings. Dr Murray relates how when Dr Crawford was married, 'he and
his wife were met at the station in a brougham which was pulled by a large party of
villagers who had turned out to welcome him home'. When he himself got married,

*...the whole village turned out and special buses were run from outside
villages and everyone enjoyed themselves and had a happy day. Even the
old village postman, who told me afterwards that he had seen me going to
the church in a car and that he had never seen me looking so sad!*

Death rituals retained a strongly communal character until well into the twentieth
century. In the 1930s, Mrs Foster performed the traditional role of laying out the dead.
Frank Spiers recalls: 'if you'd see Mrs Foster go rushing up the road, you could tell

somebody had died'. Six days was the normal period for a person to be laid out before the coffin was brought in, during which time family members and local people would file through to pay their respects. When his father died in 1934, Frank went to stay for a week with his aunt and uncle in Steppes Piece to avoid having to pass the room where his father was laid out.

The church bell was rung to announce a death in the village. During the thirties, Frank remembers, 'the death bell' was rung by Walter Smith:

If it was for a man, it was one 'dong' and wait, 'dong' and wait. Then he built it right up, 'dong, dong, dong, dong'… then bring it back. If it was a lady, he'd go 'dong, dong', 'dong, dong', take the bell up, then fetch it down again. And if it was a baby or child, there'd be three 'dongs'. Quite a few kids died. I can remember carrying a boy, Stevens. I was 13 and they had six of us schoolboys carry him. We buried him up the Grange, that angel, he was only about eight.

Dr Murray claimed responsibility for ending one village custom. When he first came to Bidford,

… it was the custom of the Doctor to attend every funeral and…it was considered his duty to walk in front of the hearse and so to speak lead the procession. This seemed to me barbaric and quite unnecessary, but I had to change the custom slowly as people in a country district are more attached to old ideas…eventually, by letting the story go around that I had been called out to something urgent, I managed to slip quite a few and so stop this bloodcurdling ritual.

Another common practice that lasted into the 1940s, and which by today's standards would be regarded as primitive, concerned post-mortems. 'In those days', recounts Dr Murray,

…we always carried out our own post-mortems…and this was always carried out if there was a sudden death …usually in the dining room or the kitchen of the deceased. The floor was covered with paper and a biscuit tin did duty to rest the head and the local policeman lent a hand…We received the magnificent sum of two guineas for three to four hours' work and the policeman got the odd two shillings for sewing up the corpse, and many a time with a young policeman he required first aid to carry him through!

A policeman's lot was not always a happy one.

Chapter 3

EARNING A LIVING

'A damned hard life'

I can remember people who worked all their life on the land until they were 65 and their hands were all crunched up. They used to go picking sprouts at four in the morning…and it was all frosted. It was a damned hard life, it really was. It's a charmed life now compared.

Rodney Crompton's recollections of Bidford highlight the continuing importance of agriculture as a means of earning a living in the forties and fifties and the demanding nature of the work involved. 'People worked so hard', recalls Betty Harris:

I remember my Mum and all the people working in the fields pea picking, plum picking and that, around where we lived. It was hard going.

Working the land

In the 1901 Census those employed in agriculture accounted for nearly 45% of the working population. Of these the main groups were 109 agricultural labourers (over 45%), 50 market gardeners (21%), 15 farmers (6%), 17 carters (7%) and nine shepherds. The agricultural depression from the mid-1870s to the mid-1890s had brought widespread unemployment among the agricultural labouring class, especially in areas of arable farming. In areas such as the Vale of Evesham, however, shifts in the balance of cultivation softened the depression's impact. Market gardening had existed in the Vale on a small scale since at least the early eighteenth century and by 1900 it had supplanted farming as the predominant form of agriculture.

Sheep washing, early twentieth century
Rodney Crompton Collection

Bidford was on the fringe of this development, but the listing of 50 market gardeners in the 1901 Census indicates that 'gardening' was well established in the parish by this period. Improved techniques in manuring and planting made the soil particularly suitable for the cultivation of fruit and vegetables. The widespread use of family labour on the smaller holdings encouraged the handing on of knowledge from one generation to the next and helped to sustain the Vale's reputation as the pre-eminent region for market gardening.

Although over 80 per cent of the agricultural labourers recorded in the 1901 Census were born within 10 miles of Bidford, itinerancy was a fact of life for many workers. Norah Hiatt recalls that her husband's parents were itinerant farm labourers, travelling round in search of work and attracted to farms where a cottage was also offered. Edward Stevens was born in rural Worcestershire and married a girl from Beoley. Their eldest child, Hannah, was born in Bromsgrove and their next two children in Grafton. By 1901 they were living in Broom.

The Trade Directories for 1900 list 12 farmers and seven market gardeners in Bidford but in 1940 only eight farmers are recorded compared with 14 market gardeners. One reason for the increase in market gardening was the policy of Warwickshire County Council after the First World War of setting up smallholdings to reward war veterans, a variation on the largely unfulfilled promise made by David Lloyd George to provide 'Homes fit for Heroes to live in'.

A unique record of market gardening from early in the century comes from the Day Book of the Bidford market gardener, Jesse Houghton. Wheat is mentioned in 1907, but from then until the record ceases in 1919, production was confined to the growing of fruit and vegetables. For much of this period plums were the dominant fruit crop and the wide variety of vegetables grown at various times included potatoes, cabbage, sprouting broccoli, broad beans, mangos, asparagus, sprouts, parsnips and onions. Jesse Houghton was typical of many small market gardeners who relied primarily on their own labour, employing additional workers only when necessary. During 1907 Walter Hendly was paid 3s 4½ d for hoeing wheat for 1½ days in April, Job Houghton received £1. 4s. 2d for moving rubbish during five days in June, and a stint of ploughing earned Mr Hall of Grafton £5.0s.0d. For others like George Holder and two of his sons in 1901, market gardening was primarily a family concern. Whether he employed additional labour is unclear, but frequent references in the Census to 'market gardeners (workers)' suggest there was a pool of labour on which larger enterprises could draw.

Arthur Stillgoe, an employee of the farmer,
Harry Smith Rodney Crompton Collection

In the 1930s much of the village was still agricultural land. Mike Paddock, who grew up on a farm in the thirties and forties, reckoned that during that time 'the vast majority of working people in Bidford were involved in agriculture'. Frank Spiers remembers there being several large farms including those of William Longford of Tower Hill and Fred Holder of Marleigh who employed about a dozen men to look after cattle. Mr George of nearby Wixford Lodge employed 20 workers and many men were employed on the Broom Court Estate. What Frank found 'surprising', however, was 'the number of people who had their own smallholdings growing fruit and vegetables'.

Producing for the market

A major factor in the expansion of smallholdings and market gardening in the Vale of Evesham during the nineteenth century was the construction of a road and rail network that linked the Vale to markets in Cheltenham, South Wales, Birmingham and beyond. Locally, the stations at Broom Junction and Bidford became focal points for the transportation of fruit and vegetables to these wider markets. As early as 1900, Jesse Houghton's plums were not only finding regular markets in Evesham and Stratford, but were also being sold in Birmingham and Manchester. Between 1915 and 1920 destinations were as distant as Glasgow and Hull.

Alan and Jack Mumford
loading fruit
Hazel Mumford Collection

The produce was put on the train at Broom Junction every Thursday and regularly reached Birmingham and Manchester about 4.00am the next day. According to George Mayrick, who was Head Porter at Broom during the 1930s, the station was a hive of commercial activity for much of the year:

In spring we would load six trucks of cabbages

from Bickmarsh Farm by 8am. Mr Fred Holder would bring us about four truckloads of garden produce each day – it went mainly to Birmingham stations or the Potteries. We'd have ten loads of hay weekly for Manchester and for firms in Birmingham. In the season there would be 20 trucks of fruit daily, often for a jam factory, and Stratford had to send us a mid-day engine to clear the one siding we had. Then in winter, there'd be sprouts and savoys.

Paddock's lorry
Mike Paddock Collection. L to R: Jack Salisbury, Mike Paddock, Tom Paddock

Lorries were increasingly used to take goods to market in Coventry, Leicester and Birmingham. For the Paddocks, lorry transport was a profitable sideline to their main farming business. In the late thirties and forties, Mike Paddock remembers going round on the lorries after school, collecting the fruit and vegetables:

[The lorries] went off at 4.30/5.00 in the morning to Coventry…In the summer when the fruit and veg was about we used to go along the bank, this side of the railway bridge, down King's Lane, by the Mill [in Broom] – we used to do that about three nights a week collecting from all the allotment holders. Most allotment holders had a couple of extra crates of cabbage or sprouts.

The Birmingham factory, Tube Equipment,

…used to have a five-ton load every week; potatoes, sprouts, apples, cabbage [and] plums for use in the factory canteen.

Such enterprise was not confined to the larger units of production. According to Frank Spiers, 'Alf Arnold would come from Alcester [to Bidford] with his horse and cart selling fruit and vegetables and buying rabbit skins for 2d'. Alternative local outlets were sought for what could not be sold at the market or from the cart. One such outlet for producers in the years after World War I was Mrs Gould's shop in the High Street. Barbara Comyns remembers:

You had to go down steps....She was very fat because it was too much bother to climb the steps. The vegetables and fruit that were sold to her looked very limp.

Some people missed no opportunity to make money. Leslie Smith recounts the story of how George Holder used to take his cauliflowers to Birmingham, but when they wouldn't sell at the price he wanted, he put them beside the road in Bidford and invited people to help themselves. This continued until a former employee of his took them and sold them in his shop.

From the early years of the century, the formation of co-operative ventures like the Littleton and Badsey Growers Society, whose membership extended as far as Bidford, provided growers with some protection against the vagaries of the market. One of the main reasons for LBG's survival was its ability to adapt to changing market demands and opportunities. Such adaptability was also evident in the case of the Paddock family. When Mike Paddock was a boy, his father's 45-50 acre farm was geared to poultry, wheat and fruit growing. Before World War II, wheat production was ended because it no longer paid. Similarly, when it became clear that 'we couldn't make a living out of fruit…we went back to pigs and poultry'. At its height, the farm owned 4 – 6,000 head of free range poultry. A lot of the eggs were originally sent to Coventry market and then to the new egg-grading station at Wixford. With an eye to the Christmas market, the farm also raised 300 or 400 turkeys ('and not many geese, thank the Lord!'). In the mid-50s, much to Mike Paddock's relief, his father got rid of the poultry to concentrate on market gardening. Mike and his brother Martin took over the running of the farm around 1965 and started growing bigger crops of everything including lettuces.

Milk and Mill

E. V. HORSEMAN
ELMFIELDS DAIRY
BIDFORD-ON-AVON

GRADE A MILK

DAILY DELIVERIES

Another business closely allied to agricultural production was dairying. Dorothy Johnson's father, Edward Horseman, established a milk business in Bidford around 1924 after recovering from shell shock sustained on the North-West Frontier of India during the war. In Dorothy's words, the business 'grew from a bucket on a bike to a very big business all around the village [and] all the villages around'. The business began accidentally. Dorothy's father used to cycle every day to collect the nearest available milk from Captain Faire's farm in Broom:

Then somebody in the lane said, 'Can you bring us some?' Then another person said, 'Can you bring us some?' So he bought a bucket and the business sort of grew and grew.

When the business became too large for him to manage on his own, he took on Percy Houghton and Charlie Thomas. Every morning Percy had to go to the Big Meadow about 5 o'clock to catch the pony that pulled the milk cart: 'It was a dreadful pony, used to bolt'.

As the business expanded, Dorothy's father bought a little van. Around 1933, 'we started to have bottles and of course bottles were a great improvement and we had to wash them'. By this time, the family had moved to the new white house built by her father in George's Elm Lane. A dairy was built in the house, the milk being kept on very cold marble slabs down some steps. The bottles had foil tops that were pressed on with a special gadget and had on them the name of the producer:

> *If you had red letters it made the milk look creamier. If you had blue letters*
> *it made it look paler. You had to splash out and have the red.*

The milk was transported in large churns in the van and delivered to Bidford and the villages round about. For some years George Cope provided competition. He had a pony and trap at the same time as Dorothy's father, 'and if there was a new customer they used to race each other'. George, however, did not buy a van and this would appear to have given her father a decisive advantage in delivering milk beyond Bidford.

Before the war Dorothy's family had no electricity, power for the dairy being provided by batteries stored in the garage. During the war however,

> *...my mother got fed up, went on the bus to Evesham, took her knitting*
> *and went to the MEB place, and said, 'I want to see the manager'. And*
> *they said, 'He's not available'...[My mother said:]'It doesn't matter. I've*
> *brought a sandwich, and I've brought my knitting and I'll stay here until*

Broom Mill in the 1980s (Margaret Nilsson Collection) + Broom Mill, early twentieth century © Warwickshire County Council PH21/59

he comes back'. So, in the end the manager came out and she said, 'We're trying to do this business in the war…and we haven't got any power and all the pubs are lit up'. In the end she persuaded him.

Italian prisoners of war were paid to dig a trench from Broom, 'all the way up the highway and…up George's Elm'.

Broom Mill provided a steady source of employment for local people until its closure in the late 1980s. The 1901 Census records six men from the parish, all residents of Broom, including the then owner, John Adkins, among the workforce. From 1916 until 1977, when it was taken over by Hemming and Son, the Mill was the property of Atkins and Thomas Ltd.

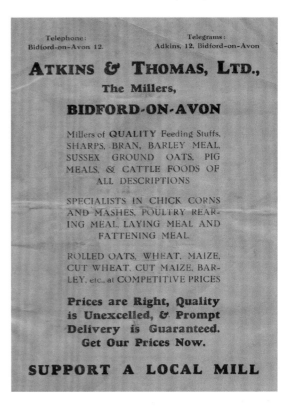

According to Frank Spiers, 'many men were employed at the Broom Flour Mill' during the 1930s and after the war.

Bricks, stone and iron

Although agriculture remained the principal source of employment for much of the twentieth century, many men earned their living in the construction trades and handicrafts. In 1901 they accounted for over 23 per cent of the working population. The largest single group within this category were the 12 men employed as platelayers and labourers on the railway. Of these ten lived in Broom, thus underlining the importance of Broom Junction in the transport network that served the parish. Platelayers were labourers, at best semi-skilled, who worked in gangs and were responsible for all aspects of track maintenance, including the replacement of worn-out rails or rotten sleepers.

In the Census 17 men were recorded as working with bricks, many of these in the brickyard owned by Edward Sill situated alongside Bidford Station. Frank Spiers reckons that there were about 40 men working in the brickyard by the 1930s and that 'most of the houses built in the village at the turn of the century, such as the ones in Icknield Street and Victoria Road, were all built with Bidford bricks'. The Brickworks continued to be a major employer until it closed during World War II. Bricklaying was a highly skilled occupation. Les Smith followed his father in the trade and after he left school went as an apprentice bricklayer in Alcester earning five shillings for a 52 ½ hour week. On leaving the army, he went back to his former job but, when told he would only receive a labourer's wage, he informed his employers that this was not good enough and that he was worth a bricklayer's wage. He got it.

Closely allied to bricklaying was stonemasonry. The most celebrated stonemason in Bidford during the twenties and thirties was William Davis who, Frank Spiers remembers, supplied most of the gravestones in the area. Fred Houghton was the skilled letter cutter, and the stones were taken out to the villages by horse and cart. Blacksmiths, a vital element in rural communities for centuries, were by the 1930s needing to diversify their work as the importance of the horse in rural life began to decline. Frank recalls that:

> *Harry Wilcox used to shoe all the horses round about. Stallions would come round all decorated in their ribbons round their neck and tail… they had to walk the stallions round because they didn't have horse boxes big enough for them in those days.*

In addition,

> *…he sharpened all the tools for Warwickshire County Council, well, the District Council mainly, and he also made hoops and hooks for us boys.*

Another respected craftsman of the same period was Percy Bryan. As well as being 'a very good painter and decorator', he was 'a super sign writer' who did all the sign writing for the pubs and local businesses.

Women at work

During the first half of the twentieth century many households could not have made ends meet without the work undertaken by their female members. Such work, of course, was in addition to the wide range of unpaid domestic tasks undertaken. One of the oldest cottage industries in the region, glove making, was still prevalent in Bidford at the beginning of the century, eight gloveresses being recorded in the 1901 Census. Although Worcester had been the centre of the trade since the middle ages, Alcester and Stratford-upon-Avon also had a long history of glove making. Women outworkers in villages like Bidford were required to work long hours for little pay making up the gloves. Increasingly, however, glove making regionally came to be concentrated in larger units of production in Worcester and, as a cottage industry, had largely died out by 1918.

Another old craft mainly undertaken by women in riverside communities was 'stripping the withies'. In Bidford the osiers, or 'withies', that grew in the osier beds near the bridge were first cut, 'stripped' of their bark, bundled together and then taken by lorry to Birmingham or wherever they were to be made into wicker baskets or cradles. During the twenties and thirties, Minnie Gardner, who 'was quite fierce and swore like a trooper', according to Peggy Griffiths, kept The Fisherman's Rest with her husband William, issued licences to fishermen and ran her own thriving business, the Osier Nates, which sold cut and bundled osiers for basket making. Not until the 1970s when the osier beds were cleared from the river did the trade die out.

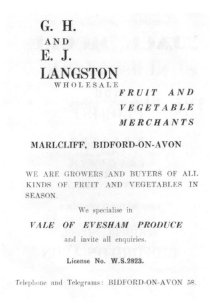

Langston's home-grown asparagus.
Barry Langston Collection

For many women, agriculture provided a ready source of employment. Ivy Webb's mother spent all her working life on the land, 'nearly all the time hoeing' on a farm at Marlcliff. While still at school, Ivy used to help with the cabbage cutting, and later worked on the threshing at Barton. Frank Spiers recalls that in the inter-war period,

> ...*many women worked when their children were at school. They found employment in pea- and bean-picking and also picking apples, plums and gooseberries. You would see them with their lovely white hats... They would push an old pram containing their food and drink for lunch along with a young baby.*

Among the older generation, Prue and Rose Edkins, those 'dear old villagers' as Peggy Griffiths describes them, would walk up the middle of the road between three or

four o'clock after a hard back-breaking day's work during pea-picking time, wearing 'what looked like masses of long black skirts, very dusty and right down to their feet'. Their large white bonnets were made of linen, 'tied under the chin, with most exquisite handiwork of tucks and frills, and starched as stiff as ram rods'.

Pea-picking at Broom.
© Warwickshire County Council PH350/250

'In service'

Apart from agricultural work, domestic service offered the most employment opportunities for young women during the first half of the century. The 1901 Census records 62 domestic servants, five of whom were male. Domestic servants accounted

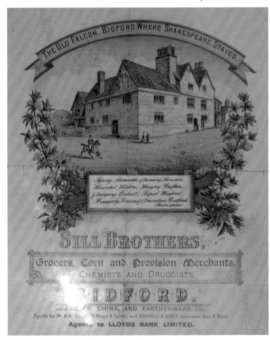

Shirley Collins Collection

for over 72 per cent of those employed in the service trades and almost 12 per cent of the total workforce. In 1901, 24 of the 34 households who kept servants employed a single domestic. A nurse, a housemaid and a cook resided at the vicarage and three servants were also employed by James Hughes at Broom Farm and Stephen Treweeks at Grange Farm. Silvester Sill, the High Street grocer and merchant, had seven servants, four of them combining work for the business with domestic duties. The majority of servants were under 20 years of age, some as young as 13 or 14.

By the 1930s, domestic service remained an important source of employment, many young women, according to Frank Spiers, going into service at the large houses of wealthy families. Such employment often provided live-in accommodation that relieved pressure on space in the servant's family home. More importantly, it gave an opportunity to girls and young women to learn household skills that equipped them for the time in later life when they would manage their own households.

Whereas for some women domestic service became a career for life, for others it was no more than a stepping-stone to other forms of employment and, as was the case with Ivy Webb, did not require 'living-in'. She went to work 'in domestic' at Cleeve Prior when she left school, doing 'anything in the way of housework' except for cooking which the family did themselves. Later she got a job in a factory in Alcester. Molly Carter's experience of domestic service was much longer. When the Head of the High School, Mr Budden, needed someone to do housework for him,

> ...nobody would volunteer, so he said, 'Does anybody want to leave before their time?' and I said 'Oh, yes'. So [at the age of 13] I went and worked for him.

After a short period with Mr Budden, she worked for 10 or 11 years as nanny at Dr Murray's in Victoria Road:

> I had to wear a kind of nurse's uniform in [the] house: in the morning it was an apron and a little cap on my head.

Over the counter

Women also found employment as shopkeepers and shop assistants. The number of and range of village shops increased between 1930 and 1960. Frank Spiers recalls that 'many local people worked in the village shops in the 1930s'. This was a time when Bidford residents still did most of their shopping in the village and most shops could count on a regular clientele who were known to them personally and whose shopping needs they were able to meet. As a result, many shops survived for a long time and provided security of employment for the shopkeepers and their assistants. The Co-op with its separate bakery, drapery, grocery and butchery departments remained a High Street landmark until 1978. Like the Co-op, James Gray's drapery business dated from the nineteenth century. As Gray and Friend's, during the 1920s and 30s, it became 'the most incredible Drapery and Millinery Emporium imaginable' according to Peggy Griffiths. During the thirties, the shop was managed by Mr and Mrs Friend and their daughter Phyllis. Peggy remembers 'the hats being quite fantastic. I often wondered if any were ever sold, I never did see any one of them being worn in the village'. Gray and Friend had closed by the end of the decade.

Small family-run shops provided family members with a settled, if modest, livelihood over several generations. The Elsmores' grocery business started in the 1880s. When James Elsmore died soon after 1900, Annie 'Grannie' Elsmore took over the business and was still in charge in 1940. By this time, recalls Peggy Griffiths:

Grand-daughter Cissie did all the fetching and carrying. I loved to watch her wield the huge butcher's knife to cut the bacon… and all the time she was serving she would be humming to herself. It must have been a very boring and dreary life.

Winnett's butchers: the meat pole is still there
Rodney Crompton Collection

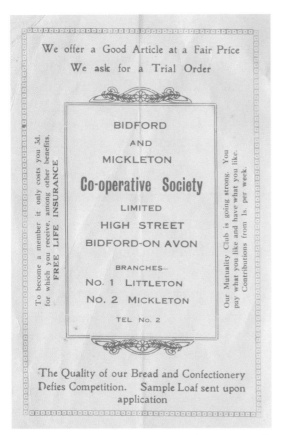

William Bennett and his wife ran a diversified family business. In the main shop, 'a veritable Aladdin's cave', according to Peggy, Mrs Bennett sold toys, postcards and every type of haberdashery. At the same time her husband was busy cutting men's hair in a room at the back, apart from when he was playing his violin.

Travelling to work

Mechanisation and the expansion of engineering and electrical trades during the inter-war years had a profound effect on employment in Bidford. One of the first businesses to reflect this development was the Canning Company set up by George Crompton in the 1920s. According to his son, Rodney, the Canning Company 'canned everything', especially strawberries and asparagus, and won a number of awards before it ran out of money. Undeterred, George set up the Reliance Bus Company in 1927 which operated as a rival to the Stratford Blue Buses between Stratford and Evesham. Rodney describes the rivalry as 'a bit like the Wild West'. The chocolate and cream coloured Reliance Buses

...used to skip one bus stop, when they knew hardly anyone would be there, with the Stratford Blue following them. They used to skip the one at The Four Alls [in Welford] and go down to the maypole stop. And so the buses were

leapfrogging each other in their competition for business.
The irony was that his father later sold out to the Stratford Blue.

Reliance Bus Company staff and buses
Rodney Crompton Collection

In the early years of the century, employment for the inhabitants of Bidford was almost wholly concentrated within the village and its environs. After World War I, an increasing number began to find work elsewhere. In the early 1930s, Frank Spiers remembers seeing 'a few men and women walking or cycling to Broom Junction to catch the train to Birmingham' and a few others 'who would cycle to Stratford and Redditch to work in the factories'. He himself, after leaving school at the age of 14 in

1939, cycled 12 miles every day to Redditch where he worked for 11 shillings a week. From there he moved to the Austin Motor Company at Longbridge until 1943 when he was called up. After completing his National Service in 1948 he was immediately offered a job again at the Longbridge Plant. He hesitated before accepting,

> *...because it was 20 miles away, but I had a motor-cycle for two years. It was hard travelling in the winter and, sliding off three times, I bought a sidecar to have three wheels.*

A near contemporary, Charlie Haywood, started work in 1945 at Black and White Garages, Harvington where he served a seven-year apprenticeship as a motor mechanic. In 1952 he was taken on at Maudslay's, popularly known as 'the factory in the forest' at Great Alne. Maudslay's had moved from Coventry in 1939 because it was regarded as a target for German bombers. When Charlie started working there, it was making axles for London buses and had over 1,000 employees. A free bus service was put on to take the men to work. Bidford alone provided nearly a full double-decker.

This trend to work outside Bidford accelerated during the fifties and sixties. By 1970 agriculture, especially market gardening, was still the main source of employment, with a few small light industrial firms, shops, banks and catering establishments providing a further 150 jobs. Already, however, a majority of the working population was finding employment in places like Evesham, Redditch and Stratford-upon-Avon. After the completion of the relief road in 1979, the light industry sector expanded with the building of the industrial estate off Waterloo Road in the early 1980s. The 2001 Census Parish Profile indicated that, despite this development, those working outside the village had risen to 76 per cent. Only a meagre four per cent were still employed in agriculture, the industry that for centuries had defined Bidford's identity more than any other.

Yesterday's Children

Chapter 4

CHILDHOOD

The Outdoor life

Rodney Crompton Collection

We were so much freer than children are today. We'd be out all day playing. We'd often walk to Ragley straight across the fields and then come back, crossing the Weir at Broom as a short cut, and not be back until after dark and our parents didn't know where we were…

Much of the freedom referred to by Rodney Crompton, when recalling his forties' childhood, was enjoyed in and around the River Avon.

The river was our swimming pool. We swam every day.

Fishing was popular but the Avon was also the source of more adventurous pursuits as Rodney's older sister, Marjorie Kidson, recalled:

A little way down from the bridge there was an island in the river, willow trees grew on the island and they were harvested. There was a plank from the river bank to the willows and I used to walk across it to the island. When my parents found out, I was in trouble.

Rodney was more daring than his sister:

> *We used to make reed rafts, wrap our arms around them and float down the river. You had to get down to the bridge but it was dangerous as there was a big hole on the other side.*

When Rodney was a child, Bidford was surrounded by fields and woodland, and the relative absence of traffic made the streets a popular place for recreation:

> *A gang of us played' tin can Tommy' and put a tin in the middle of the road. You had to go out hunting to catch people and if anyone could sneak in and kick the can away while you were not there, then everyone runs away.*

According to Frank Spiers, the street games continued after dark:

> *We used to play marbles...we played a lot under the gaslight on the corner here...about thirty of us...and we'd play conkers. Harry Wilcox (the blacksmith) made us a hoop...and we used to play with that.*

Football was one game not played in the street, 'cause if the ball went over into Miss Holder's...oh dear!' There was, however, no shortage of safe open space for football and other games:

> *The Co-op field was a good field, where Saxonfields is now. The back of the Catholic Church and Quinney's Court was all one big field so we'd play there. Another place where we played was where Crompton Avenue is now as that was all fields.*

As well as football, Frank remembers playing hopscotch and skipping, whilst safety mattered little to Rodney and his friends:

> *We used to do chariot racing with pushbikes, one on a bike and the other one hanging on the back on roller skates, down Marriage Hill.*

Despite these hairy escapades, however:

> *I don't think any of us were killed or drowned. One kid, who was a stranger, got knocked over in the High Street; and an evacuee was drowned in the river, but by and large we all survived.*

Long walks were common amongst children from all backgrounds. In 'Sisters by a River' Barbara Comyns remembers:

> *Our governesses used to take us for walks every day...We called the walk to Barton the fairy way because there were so many blackthorn bushes all sparkling with blossom in the Spring...The governesses were rather fond of this walk as there were no hills to climb...they didn't like taking us to Marlcliff much because we used to go mad when we got there and slide down the cliffs and ruin our knickers.*

On Sundays over a decade later, Frank Spiers remembers walking round Marlcliff, Cleeve Prior and Salford with half a dozen other children:

> *If we hadn't got time to do that we'd go round Marlcliff or we'd go round Barton or we'd go up George's Elm Lane...there'd be nothing else to do.*

Also out for a walk on Sundays was Dorothy Johnson:

> *Every Sunday afternoon we used to go for a walk with my mother because my father wanted to sleep or garden. We used to walk up the lane and out by the Three Horseshoes pub in Wixford and back ...We used to do a good many miles.*

It is clear from oral evidence that the outdoor life and the greater freedom it provided was an experience common to most Bidford children during the thirties and forties. Homes offered not only fewer facilities for play and recreation but also, like school, a more controlled environment.

Educating 'Yesterday's Children'

When the twentieth century dawned, the Anglican Church held a near monopoly of education in Bidford. In an age of fierce denominational rivalry, the National Society was set up in 1811 to provide elementary education for the poor in accordance with 'the Principles of the Established Church'. A small National School, built in Church Street, was enlarged in 1846 to accommodate 160 children. Over a century later this building was to become the present-day Church Hall. As the population increased, the pressure on accommodation intensified and in 1872, according to White's Directory, 'a large and neat National School with a house for the master, was erected...on the Broom Road'. The 'Old School', as it was known, continued to be used as an Infant Department until 1950.

Infant voices

The Infant Department had an average attendance of 80 in 1900, according to Kelly's Directory, and was run by Miss Mary Poole. By the 1920s Mrs Warner, wife of the Junior School Head, Arthur Warner, was in charge, assisted by Miss Smith. Mollie Henderson started school in 1921:

> *I can remember my first day as a very shy four and a half year old. I had a dark red velvet dress with a starched pinafore over it and new brown boots which my mother had buttoned up the sides with a button hook which I still have. I didn't really want to go to school, I was happy at home amongst*

all our animals, cows, horses, pigs, poultry, cats and dogs, so it was with a very heavy heart that I went clutching my mother's hand.

Infants School, 1931 (Frank Spiers Collection)
Front Row L to R : J Clee, n/k, A Harris, T Craven, B Moore, C Bennett
2nd Row L to R: J Smith, D Mayrick, B Manders, D Bailey, J Gailey, R King, A Bateman, P Edkins, M Dance, P Bryan, J Mills, W Hands, H Dance, F Clee
3rd Row L to R: G Gould, N Edkins, n/k, M Swift, V Pulham, S Harper, N Foster, N Harris, n/k, E Sherwood, F Bennett, N Teale, E Langston, E Morrel, B Gould
Back Row L to R: D Bott, S Baldwin, K Prickett, G Craven, E Osbourne, F Spiers, D Bateman, G Higley, D Liddell, J Green, n/k F Bennett, L Gould
Teachers: Left Miss Smith, Right Miss Jackson

Charlie Haywood started school over 10 years later. The school day began 'with assembly with both classes singing a hymn and saying prayers. Then the screen was closed, dividing school into two classrooms'. Instruction in the three 'Rs' (reading, 'riting and 'rithmetic) was at the heart of the curriculum. Mollie Henderson 'had those lovely books "A is for Apple" and we soon learnt our ABC and to count to 10 on a large abacus'. Spelling was taken very seriously. One memory that has lived with Frank Spiers for over 80 years 'was having to write "said" 100 times after spelling it "sed"'.

The children's classroom experience, however, extended well beyond the three 'Rs', as Mollie Henderson lovingly recalled:

> *Mrs Warner was very good at organising singing and dancing. She had quite a few tall Welsh hats and wraps and we all loved getting dressed up and dancing in the costumes.*

Dinah Holder, who started school at the age of four in 1927, was similarly positive:

> *At the age of six I can remember we had an orchestra, it was a band really.*
> *I was made Band Master, I had to wear a suit, had a music stand, stood on*
> *a box with a baton. I thought I was the cat's whiskers!*

A period of rest was a daily feature of afternoon school. Charlie Haywood recalls:

> *After we had eaten our sandwiches and had a play outside, we were …*
> *made to lie down on straw mats for a rest. Presumably to re-charge our*
> *batteries, after all we were only five years old and for many of us, this was*
> *the longest time we had been away from our parents.*

This practice, referred to by Mollie Henderson as 'Heads Down', involved 'folding our arms and resting our heads for about 15 minutes, sometimes some of us actually went to sleep!'

The 'Big School'

Junior School, 1914 © Warwickshire County Council PH352/30/93

Transfer at the age of seven to the 'Big School' in Victoria Road marked the next stage of schooling for village children. For the vast majority, until the Secondary School was built in 1938, it was also their last. Until 1918, when the leaving age was raised to 14, many children left school as early as 12.

As well as Arithmetic, English, History and Geography, Frank Spiers listed PT and Gardening as the main subjects in the curriculum. Les Smith recalled that the school had a number of allotments at the foot of Marriage Hill which were split up into plots for the boys to work for one or two periods a week. In a community where, in the 1930s, market gardening offered plentiful employment opportunities, the hours the boys spent on the allotment provided relevant training for life after school.

While the boys worked in the garden, the girls learned domestic skills such as needlework and knitting. The latter was not a happy memory for Norah Hiatt and her friend Mary Bennett:

> *12 months we were knitting a matinee coat between us. We done it one afternoon, and next afternoon we had to take it out, and when we left school we never finished it…I always said I would never touch another piece of knitting…I used to pay to have my babies' clothes knitted.*

For Frank Spiers and his sister Dinah Holder extra-curricular activities provided some of the more memorable moments of their years at the 'Big School'. Frank enjoyed the drama productions that the Head, Mr Warner, put on in Class 6 and 7:

> *Mr Warner…was a good amateur actor. This rubbed off on his pupils and every year we performed plays in the Co-op Hall. [He] would write the play on the blackboard and we would copy it into our books then learn the words.*

Day trips to Liverpool and the Mersey Tunnel, Bristol and London were the highlights of Class 6 and 7 for Dinah. An incident that occurred on one of these outings influenced her behaviour for life:

> *When we had our picnic, some boys and girls fetched cups of tea for all, but the boys had put salt in the cups instead of sugar which made us all sick, not a good joke. I've never had sugar since.*

Although Frank and Dinah were able to recite the names of all their Junior school teachers, Norah Hiatt and Charlie Haywood had a special mention for 'Gertie' Armitage who spent all her teaching career at the school prior to her retirement in 1945. Charlie remembers that:

> *She was good at getting us to do our work and used to walk around the classroom looking over shoulders to see what you were doing, and occasionally she would come with the remark, 'Now then, who's letting off the perfume, then?' which had the effect of reducing the whole class into fits of laughter.*

The private sphere

A small minority of children in Bidford was educated privately, and the evidence would suggest that even fewer had governesses. During the nineteenth and early twentieth centuries the live-in governess, not to be confused with the more child-minding nanny, was a common feature of many middle class households. Governesses were often spinsters of variable age, generally from middle class backgrounds themselves. Barbara Comyns, who was born in 1909, endured a succession of governesses during her childhood at Bell Court. The least popular was the 70 year old Miss Vann who had 'always been in the best families'. All the children hated her:

> *I got a smacked bottom every night…in case I talked to Beatrix instead of going to sleep…One day, she dragged me upstairs to put me to bed for a punishment, but when we reached the top of the stairs I suddenly thought I couldn't stand all these punishments any more and before I hardly knew what I'd done I'd kicked her down the stairs, she went down head first and landed with her head in a kind of brass pot that lived at the bottom…then she lay quite still…I thought she [was] dead so I crawled away and hid under a bed…When they found me a few hours later no one was cross… not even Miss Vann…She left soon after this, she said we were getting too old for her.*

The much younger Miss Glide followed Miss Vann. A popular village figure and in great demand at tennis parties and dances, she stayed for several years before leaving to get married. Although she was not a particularly good teacher,

> *…she tried to make the lessons interesting, she was the first governess who read to us in the evenings and seemed to enjoy taking us for walks and playing games with us.*

The alternative to a live-in governess was the small private school. By 1919 Barbara and her sisters had been without a governess for some time, with the result that:

> *Daddy and several other local parents …thought it would be a good idea to start a small private school…two rooms in a villa on the Gorse [Broom] Road were taken and a teacher called Miss Jones was engaged.*

Miss Jones was Welsh, wore pince-nez glasses 'and resembled a goat in nearly every respect'. There were only eight pupils, Barbara being the eldest. She 'found lessons very easy and dull, the other children seemed to be bored too and often went to sleep, so did Miss Jones'. After two terms Miss Jones was declared 'unsuitable' and the school closed down.

Miss Grove's School, 1927 (Dorothy Johnson Collection)
Front Row L to R: Jean Hobbs, ? Phillips, Joan Griffiths, Anne Aspinwall, Sheila Derrick, ?
Phillips, Dorothy Horseman, Kenneth Evans.
Middle Row L to R: Brian Hughes, Brian Jakeman, John Johnson.
Back Row L to R: Margaret Hughes, (Teacher) Florence Grove, Jimmy Lovegrove, Barbara
Jakeman, Betty Griffiths, Phyllis Horseman, Roger Johnson.

During the 1920s Miss Florence Grove started the only recorded private school in
Bidford on the upper floor of the Assembly Rooms. Dorothy Johnson's elder sister,
Phyllis, was a pupil there. By the time Dorothy herself was old enough, the school
had moved to a big house on the opposite side of the road:

> *It was just one room, to me as a four year old, it was huge...there were
> about seventeen of us.*

Miss Grove acknowledged that the education provided was not the best preparation for
anyone aspiring to a Grammar School education. After Dorothy's sister failed to win
a scholarship to Alcester Grammar School, Miss Grove advised their father: "'What
you really need to do is to send [Dorothy] to an elementary school, you'll stand a
better chance'". Dorothy's father, however, did not like Mr Warner, the Headmaster of
Bidford School, so she went to Stratford 'to the school opposite the hospital' and duly
won a scholarship to Alcester Grammar.

Secondary experiences

During the first quarter of the century, 'secondary' education was outside the reach of most children, their families being unable to afford private school fees and grammar school scholarships being limited in number. By the 1920s, however, there was a widespread recognition of the economic and social benefits to be gained from establishing a national system of secondary education. From 1928 onwards, it became government policy to transfer pupils to a 'secondary' school at the age of 11 and to rename the old elementary schools 'Primary' schools. In many rural communities such as Bidford however, transfer did not take place for a decade or more, largely because the building programme was slowed by the economic depression.

When the School in Victoria Road opened on Monday 25 April 1938, 118 children were admitted, 73 of them transfers from Bidford Primary School. One of these was Frank Spiers who became the first Head Boy of the School before leaving twelve months later.

Any hopes that the School routine might be free of disruption during its early years of development were dashed with the outbreak of war in September 1939 and the arrival of evacuees. This was part of 'Operation Pied Piper', the Government's plan to move children from towns and cities in danger from enemy bombing to the relative security of the countryside. By the end of the year 10 evacuees, all but one from the Birmingham area, had been admitted to the School, but the major influx followed the Coventry blitz on 14 November 1940. In the School Log Book for 18 November, the Head, Ernest Budden, noted that 66 children from Coventry were received. On 25 November a further 69 evacuees joined them. Faced with this emergency, the School remained open during the Christmas holidays in order to provide additional teaching for the Coventry children. Some evacuees returned home within a month, but when the School reopened in January 1941, evacuees from Coventry and Birmingham accounted for 105 of the 232 children on the roll. Thereafter, the proportion steadily fell.

As well as having to cope with the problems of integrating evacuee children, the School had to take other extraordinary measures during the war years. According to the Managers' Minutes, the teaching of woodwork was abandoned 'as a wartime necessity' and replaced by Garden construction and Engineering. A course on tractor driving, maintenance and repair was also taken by the older boys, and neighbouring farmers 'greatly appreciated the boys' services' during harvesting.

Despite these unsettled times, the Managers' Minutes reported His Majesty's Inspectors 'highly satisfied' with the work of the School on their visits in 1942 and 1943. Charlie Haywood, a pupil from 1940 – 41 before transferring to Alcester Grammar School, was equally satisfied:

> *[I] enjoyed the time there very much. It was rather strange at first to have different teachers for the lessons…My favourite subject was metalwork closely followed by games, especially football. There was great rivalry between the four houses, Shakespeare, Eliot, Dugdale and Drayton. Everyone was really keen to earn points to win the School Shield for their house at the end of the year. Points were awarded for good class work, being punctual and good behaviour.*

Extra-curricular activities were a regular feature of the School from the outset. Educational visits were normally undertaken at the end of the summer term. In July 1938 the Log Book recorded that '71 children under the charge of Mr Noise, Mr Stratford and Mrs Keytes visited [the] Shakespeare Memorial Theatre to see Macbeth'. Arthur Savage, who succeeded Mr Budden in June 1947, reported to the Governors the following April that he hoped an outing to Bristol in July would include a visit to a tobacco factory. Betty Harris, who started at the school in 1948, has fond memories of one particular extra-curricular activity:

> *Twice a week if anyone was interested, [the sports master] would teach us ballroom dancing in the Hall. That was very popular; he was very charming! I remember the song 'Charmaine' - that was the waltz. We learned to waltz, quickstep, foxtrot. We didn't have to pay for dancing lessons like some people.*

Bidford High School Brian Cobb Collection

Sport was popular with both sexes. Betty Harris loved hockey, netball and athletics, especially the high jump and the relay. The relay team participated in the South Warwickshire sports and the all-Warwickshire event:

> *Bearing in mind we were just a small school we did really well. It was a very good standard…we all liked it. We got quite a lot of firsts.*

Football fortunes varied over the years but the school team went through the whole of the 1955/56 season without losing a single game, scoring 64 goals and conceding only 14.

Throughout the forties and fifties, the School received very positive reports from HM Inspectors. In 1949 they found 'a smoothly running organisation', 'very good' discipline and 'sincere and devoted' teaching, 'though the standard of achievement is not high in the subjects of formal instruction'. According to the report in December 1956, 'excellent work was being consistently carried out by the staff'. Betty Harris echoed the Inspectors' view:

> *It was a very good school…Discipline was excellent and they were very fair. I was always a giggler, giggling in the wrong place! I wasn't a brilliant scholar, just average, but I enjoyed school. Some of the teachers were very interesting. I liked geography and history. You learned an awful lot; I think it was the way we were taught.*

Alcester Grammar School provided the main alternative form of secondary education for a minority of Bidford children. Most entrants, like Dorothy Johnson in 1935, secured their place by passing the scholarship examination, but some, like Dorothy's elder sister, Phyllis, had to pay fees to gain entrance. Their father, Edward Horseman, was adamant: '"They've both got to go. One can't go without the other"'. His determination that both his daughters should receive a grammar school education, Dorothy recalls, placed a strain on the family's finances: 'He was struggling. My brother was a baby. He was working at the business'.

A close friend, Marjorie Kidson, also passed the scholarship and remembers cycling the four miles to Alcester with Dorothy and Phyllis: 'No buses then, but we all survived it'. Marjorie went on to become Head Girl at the Grammar School and later taught there. At a time when most Grammar Schools remained single-sex schools, Alcester Grammar admitted boys and girls. However, according to Dorothy Johnson, girls were expected to be 'ladylike' in their behaviour, and 'on sports days we didn't do sports [athletics], we did arts and craft'. This disappointed Dorothy, who loved all sports and was captain of the girls' tennis, hockey and netball teams, but 'it was just one of those things, you just accepted it'. After leaving school Dorothy pursued a teaching career and was Head Mistress of Bidford Infant School from 1964 to 1980.

Mike Paddock was at the Grammar School from 1944-50, by which time a bus service was provided to take pupils from Bidford to Alcester. He described the School as 'very good' even if he did manage to get on the wrong side of the Physics and Chemistry teachers: 'I was particularly in trouble with them'.

'Spare the rod'

In a small village like Bidford during the thirties and forties, everyone knew everyone, with the result that news, especially news of misbehaviour, travelled quickly. As Charlie Haywood reflected:

> The one big mystery during our schooldays was the 'village grapevine', we never managed to find out how it worked. If we had been up to mischief or had had the cane, how come our parents always knew about it before we got back home?

Discipline exercised by the arm of the law was also strict. All children, according to Frank Spiers, were afraid of the village policeman, PC Bill Munday:

> If you did anything wrong he would put you in the police cell for a couple of hours!

Rodney Crompton recalled how

> ...he used to take a swing at you with his cloak which used to weigh about 10 pounds! He would give you a thick ear if he could!

All those interviewed testified to the rigorous discipline they encountered at each stage of their schooling. Charlie Haywood discovered this discipline very early:

> The first day at [Infant] school was quite a shock to many of us, discipline was very strict, as I found to my cost...We were told to keep quiet but to no avail... For no particular reason I was ordered to the front of the class and made to stand in the corner for the rest of the lesson. Such shame, but it taught me to keep my mouth closed unless spoken to.

Charlie recalled one incident which showed that teachers had no compunction about punishing the whole class for the misdeeds of the few:

> The lavatory doors to remove the buckets in the girls' loo when full were in the wall of our loo and were fastened with a sliding bolt, there being no flush toilets. Someone, needless to say not me, found that by opening the doors it was possible to tickle the girls' bottoms with a long piece of grass. This came to a stop when one boy used a stinging nettle instead of grass! When this came to the teacher's attention, no one would admit to being involved – in those days everyone stuck together and kept quiet...

The consequence of this was detention and all the boys had to stay in for a week during playtime.

Mike Paddock was always in trouble:

I had the cane on the first day I was there. I had a whack across the knuckles because I broke a pencil and I had a whack on the last day there.

Charlie Haywood approached his move to the Junior School with trepidation after 'friends who were already there told us that if we thought the Infant School was strict, just wait till you get here'. However, the warning went unheeded:

Just the same as my first day in the Infants School, I was unfortunate enough to be caught talking. Mrs Warner (the teacher) had eyes in the back of her head and immediately picked me out as the culprit. This time the punishment was more severe. I had to stand on a chair and have the backs of my legs smacked.

Worse was to come, since the embodiment of strict discipline, the Head Master, Mr Warner, awaited Charlie in the top class:

If he found you were not paying attention to what he was saying, a piece of chalk and sometimes the blackboard rubber was thrown with great accuracy at the offender. He was rather adept at using the cane which, in this case, was an old army cane with a silver ferule on one end.

Mr Warner was not averse to making the innocent suffer as well as the miscreants. Charlie vividly remembered the incident in 1937 when a Blenheim bomber made a forced landing at the top of Tower Hill:

The whole school was called together and Mr Warner gave strict instructions that no one was to go anywhere near it. Just imagine it – the only planes we had seen were high in the sky and now we had one on the ground virtually on our doorstep…The temptation was too much for us, especially us boys… Mr Warner somehow found out the names of the boys he definitely knew had disobeyed his orders and they were caned. The rest of us were kept in at playtimes just in case we were guilty!

Mike Paddock, who was caned by Mr Warner 'at least once a week', remembers him with dread:

He was a real sadist he was! I can remember two or three young pupils having their fingers broken by him with the cane.

Charlie Haywood on the other hand was less critical:

I wouldn't want people to get the wrong idea about Mr Warner, he was hard and strict with us but he was fair. If you got punished you probably deserved it.

When Mr Warner retired in July 1946 after 29 years at the School, he defended his regime of strictness in a letter to the Parish Magazine:

I have had many things said to me, and about me, not all of them complimentary. Indeed, one man, many years ago, expressed the pious wish that my house might burn down... I have, at times, been looked upon as Bidford's Public Enemy No.1 but I have... done what I considered to be my duty [and it has been gratifying] to meet as men, many who as boys under me, having perhaps made the acquaintance of the' instrument' of my discipline, seem to me to be little the worse for the treatment.

Chapter 5

TIME OFF

'Drunken Bidford'?

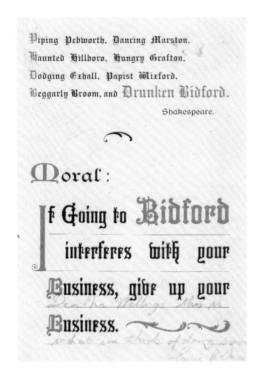

Piping Pebworth, Dancing Marston.
Haunted Hillboro, Hungry Grafton.
Dodging Exhall, Papist Wixford.
Beggarly Broom, and Drunken Bidford.

Shakespeare.

Moral:

If Going to Bidford interferes with your Business, give up your Business.

The ways in which the people of Bidford spent their 'time off' from work and domestic responsibilities took many forms. One popular leisure venue was the public house. In 1901, there were six public houses in the village serving a population of 1,369: the White Lion, the Boot, the Mason's Arms, the Pleasure Boat, the Plough and the Bull's Head. By 1903 the Boot had changed its name to the Fisherman's Rest. All survived into the second half of the century. Some families, such as the Gardners at the Fisherman's Rest, the Holders at the Mason's Arms, and the Spiers family at the Bull's Head, held the licence for long periods. The link between the Spiers family and the Bull's Head stretched back more than 140 years and only ended with Fred Spiers' retirement in the 1990s.

PLEASURE BOAT INN, BIDFORD-ON-AVON

BOATS and PUNTS for Hire by Hour or Day

ANSELL'S Finest ALES, WINES and STOUTS.

CHOPS and STEAKS at the Shortest Notice.

Luncheons and Teas.

Phone 52.

Large and Small Parties Catered for.

C. WILSHAW, PROPRIETRESS (late Soho Road, BIRMINGHAM).

Home Fed Ham and Egg Teas a Speciality.

Rodney Crompton Collection

Public houses in the inter-war period operated under strict regulation. On weekdays opening hours were from 10.00am to 2.00pm and from 6.00 to 10.00pm, whilst Sunday opening was limited to two hours from noon to 2.00pm. According to Frank Spiers, PC Munday regularly came round all the Bidford pubs,

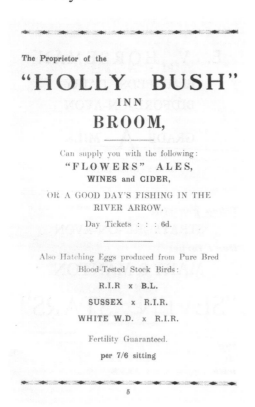

The Proprietor of the

"HOLLY BUSH"

INN

BROOM,

Can supply you with the following:

"FLOWERS" ALES,
WINES and CIDER,

OR A GOOD DAY'S FISHING IN THE
RIVER ARROW.

Day Tickets : : : 6d.

Also Hatching Eggs produced from Pure Bred
Blood-Tested Stock Birds:

R.I.R x B.L.

SUSSEX x R.I.R.

WHITE W.D. x R.I.R.

Fertility Guaranteed.

per 7/6 sitting

5

especially during the evening, to check that licensing hours were being adhered to. Frank claims there was little or no drunkenness inside or outside the pubs, though he does admit to seeing the draymen and the dustmen often 'spark out' on the lawn behind the Bull's Head sleeping off a hangover. Inside, his mother Victoria refused to serve anyone who was judged to have had too much to drink and PC Munday dealt with any disorder by putting the offenders in the cell for the night.

Rodney Crompton remembers rowdy visits to village pubs during the war by bomber crews from Honeybourne and Long Marston, but after the war rowdiness was largely confined to the pea-picking and plum-picking season when casual workers, many of them 'gypsies', poured into the village.

During the early part of the century pubs were largely male preserves, but as a child Frank Spiers remembers a few women accompanying their husbands, and individual women like old Maud Seymour, a World War I widow, who came every night to the Bull's Head for her glass of stout and a bit of company. Entertainment and competitions were regularly available. At the Bull's Head the Saturday night sing-song round the piano proved very popular and pub games such as crib, dominoes, shove-halfpenny, quoits and skittles were played every evening during the week. Darts did not appear at the Bull's Head until 1935. The first dartboard, according to Frank Spiers, was made of plasticine which had to be rolled each evening. The game quickly caught on and within a few years the Bull's Head had one of the best darts teams among the village pubs and was competing successfully in the Stratford Darts League. After World War II Ladies Darts and Dominoes leagues were also established. Molly Carter played in the Ladies Darts Team at the Pleasure Boat: 'I used to love dart playing'. When her future husband Bill visited her house the first time, as arranged, he found nobody at home since Molly was down at the Pleasure Boat playing darts.

Pubs arranged family outings. Stretching from the 1930s to the 1960s, the outings from the Bull's Head included visits to the Aldershot and Tidworth Military Tattoos, race meetings at Royal Ascot and Hurst Park, athletics at the White City, pantomime at the Coventry Hippodrome and variety at the London Palladium. Sometimes pubs served as sources of vital information. Frank recalls that in the years when few homes owned a wireless, men unwilling to wait until 8.00pm for the Sports Argus would come to the Bull's Head at six o'clock on a Saturday evening armed with pencil and paper to take down the football results.

'A River Resort'

Rodney Crompton Collection

Rodney Crompton Collection

From the late nineteenth century onwards Bidford could truly be described as 'a river resort'. The November edition of the Parish Magazine for 1901 referred to 'the hundreds and at certain times thousands' of visitors who poured into Bidford during the summer months. It was not until the 1970s, with the rapid growth in car ownership, the advent of the package holiday and the appeal of more exotic locations that the village's tourist trade began to decline.

Until the rail closures of the late 1940s, this trade was facilitated by the railway network linking Bidford with large centres of population such as Birmingham and the Black Country. Bidford was within easy walking distance from Salford Priors station and

Rodney Crompton recalls how as a boy he would stand in front of his father's garage on the Salford Road on a Saturday and watch what looked 'like a row of ants coming down the hill from Salford Station'.

Bridge and charabanc, 1916 Rodney Crompton Collection

Increasingly important were the charabancs and coaches that brought growing numbers of trippers into the village. Until 1937 when holidays with pay became a legal requirement, many working people could not afford to take more than one or two days' holiday, and a pleasant day's excursion from Birmingham to riverside villages like Bidford was an attractive proposition. At the same time, Bidford's desire to attract the wealthy and respectable as well as the lower classes was evident from coloured postcards from the first decade of the century, featuring smart, fashionably dressed ladies.

One of Bidford's major attractions was 'Daddy' Holland's Pleasure Grounds. For nearly half a century, until he was forced to shut down his business during World War II because of a shortage of fuel for the boats, William Holland's Pleasure Grounds became a magnet for visitors and locals alike. Peggy Griffiths had happy memories of her visits there:

> *Whenever I could get away [from the Post Office] for an hour I would take my small daughter, in her pushchair, to these delightful gardens. There were several double wooden swingboats, prettily painted, a small*

HOLLAND'S PLEASURE GROUNDS, BIDFORD-ON-AVON.

Boating on the River Avon Rodney Crompton Collection

HOLLAND'S LARGE PAVILION, BIDFORD ON AVON.

roundabout and a tea shop. This latter was managed by two of Mr Holland's sisters, Mrs Dalton and Mrs Hammond.

The steamer trips under Captain 'Skipper' Jones were especially popular. For Marjorie Kidson :

One of the nice trips we had was on one of those Holland's boats down the river to Cleeve Prior. When you got there it was off the boat and into the café. If you fancied it you could walk along the plank across the river. There was only a metal rail to hold onto on our side and nothing on the other. Changing places was fraught with difficulty but I don't remember anyone falling in.

Audrie Spiers Collection

The novelist Barbara Comyns, writing as an impressionable child, prone to exaggeration, painted a very negative picture of visitors to Bidford in the years following World War I:

> *Awful people called trippers used to come to our village on Public Holidays in the Summer…They hired boats from Holland's…They couldn't row or punt, but splashed, screamed, showed their braces and got drunk, they sweated and got sick and fell in the river, we didn't help them out with a boat hook, we just hoped they would drown, sometimes they did…Maybe we were rather hard on the trippers, but they really were beastly and were always giving the village girls babies and making an awful noise, the babies as well as the trippers.*

The enforced closure of the Pleasure Grounds during World War II marked the end of an era. 'Daddy' Holland gave up the boat trips, the tea shop closed down and he turned his hand to producing battery chickens which covered the boatyard and the landing stages. For some years he also kept exotic ornamental fowls in large cages. Finally, when he could no longer manage to look after the birds, he sold the land. Despite the demise of the Pleasure Grounds, boat hire and boat trips remained a crucial part of Bidford's continuing appeal. Bidford Boats is still in business today.

Carnival time

Bidford's tourist appeal also owed much to the development of the Big Meadow as a leisure amenity after the Second World War. Before then, the 'Big Meadow' was no more than the name implied, a large field with long grass and cattle grazing on it, a place where local residents, like Dorothy Johnson's family, kept their ponies. It was little used for public recreation other than on sports and carnival days. After the war however, the Parish Council Minutes reveal how it became a regular site for Kimberley's fun fairs at Whitsun, Trinity and August Carnival week. A coaster slide was installed, football, cricket and hockey pitches were created and the Birmingham Angling Association was granted fishing rights on the meadow bank of the river.

Rodney Crompton Collection

The annual August Bank Holiday Carnival, which dates from the 1930s, drew crowds of visitors to the Big Meadow. Mary Paddock remembers the crowds coming by train to Bidford on Carnival day: 'You could hardly walk, there were so many people'. This was an essentially local event however, organised by and for the inhabitants of Bidford and central to the village's sense of identity as a community. Frank Spiers remembers the Carnival procession through the village and how he and other children used to dress up and walk behind a Brass Band from Alcester or Bretforton, with the floats decked out on small lorries or more often on decorated carts drawn by horses. Pride of place went to the Carnival Queen, the first of whom was Betty Gowers. Before it moved to the Big Meadow the Carnival was held on the meadow on the opposite side of the bridge. There were athletics events for all ages and a gymkhana organised for several years by Miss Longford of Tower Hill farm, who, Frank Spiers recalls, 'always rode side saddle, dressed in a long skirt and wore a top hat'.

Carnival time in the 1950s © Evesham Journal

The Carnival became a much smaller scale event during the war years, but was then revived in 1947 to raise money to build the Crawford Hall. In 1949 the Parish Magazine noted that 'Bidford was very much alive during Carnival week…One of the outstanding features was the floodlighting of our ancient Parish Church'. The following year an estimated 6,000 people attended the Carnival. Once the Crawford Hall had been completed in 1955 however, enthusiasm for the Carnival waned and Bidford had no Carnival during most of the sixties.

In 1970, at Frank Spiers' instigation, the Carnival was revived to raise money for a new Sports Pavilion on the Big Meadow. Businessmen responded enthusiastically to Frank's request for sponsorship. He relates how he was helping his brother Fred one night in the Bull's Head when a customer came up to him and said, '"Frank, I am going to sponsor you for £1000". I could not believe it'. On the morning of the Carnival:

> …as early as 7.00am Martin and Michael Paddock with their tractor with a dozen other men would be putting all the tea tents, marquees and stalls up, ready for the WI Ladies with their lovely teas, the Mothers' Union with their cake stall. The Churchmen would be on the gate at nine o'clock because people came early in their cars to have a lovely day by the river… Tommy Wilson brought a good fair from Redditch and was very generous to us.

The Paddock family float, 1970s Photograph courtesy of The Alcester Chronicle

One of the highlights of the newly revived Carnival in which Frank regularly took part was the Pram Race:

> *About 20 of us men with a lighter man in a pram would race from the Bull's Head up street along Waterloo Road to Broom, drink a pint of beer at Broom Tavern, then carry on through Broom down Victoria Road to the Pleasure Boat, have another pint, then run up the High Street finishing at the Bull's Head. The crowds of people in Broom, Victoria Road and all up the High Street were terrific, it kept us going.*

The Carnival remained popular throughout the eighties but died out during the next decade, as a result of dwindling support.

Church and Chapel

One of the centres of community life was the mediaeval Parish Church of St Laurence. A chapel of ease in Broom in 1878 consolidated Anglican influence in the parish and the only challenge to Anglican dominance in the village during the nineteenth century came from the Wesleyan Methodists. A chapel was built in Chapel Lane in 1801 and enlarged in 1837. The long-established Catholic tradition associated with Salford Hall came to an end in 1948 when the chapel was declared unsafe for public worship, prompting the local Roman Catholic community to raise funds to purchase a building in Quinney's Lane, Bidford. The building, previously a builder's workshop, was converted into the church of St Joseph the Worker and opened in 1960.

Methodist Chapel, 1981 Jo Sawtell Collection

The Parish Church offered a range of activities and commitments. The Rev Albert Harrison was appointed in 1932, and during the early years of his ministry congregations and the number of communicants markedly increased. Frank Spiers remembers the Church being full for Evensong in the years before the War, 'because it was somewhere to go'. There were no televisions and some people 'hadn't got wirelesses'. Finding a seat was not always easy, not least because many of the old box pews were either owned or rented by members of the congregation, a practice common to many churches at the time. Frank recalls that from his seat in the choir stalls he could only see the heads of those sitting in the box pews:

> *When some people came in and took somebody's pew they'd turf 'em out you know! Me Uncle Charlie and me Auntie Maud and Mrs Drinkwater, they'd got their own pew and woe betide you if you went in it!*

The 1930s were a golden age for the Bidford Church Choir, the Boys' Choir winning first prize at the Leamington Music Festival on no less than six successive occasions. The full Choir also carried off its share of awards, twice winning first prize. These successes owed much to the talent and dedication of the young Choirmaster, Jack Styles. Frank Spiers, who joined the Choir at the age of five in 1930, recalls how Styles cycled over to Bidford from Stratford every Tuesday evening to rehearse the Boys Choir:

Then on a Friday night he'd take us boys first and then the whole Choir would come, the boys and the six women and twelve men. Oh he was ever so good…he used to pay for us to go to the theatre to see a pantomime…He used to get football matches up against Stratford choir boys [and] against Alveston Choir boys.

The choirboys wore 'Eton Collars', which were sent to Stratford laundry to be washed and starched. Rodney Crompton also had great respect for Mr Styles, whom he described as 'quite a disciplinarian', but he recalls that the singing at Sunday services did not always produce the togetherness characteristic of the Festival competitions:

One of the male choir members with a very strong voice sometimes lost track of the music! It was wonderful to hear the conflict between the congregation and the Choir! Some of them were following him and some of them the Choir!

In 1946 the Boys Choir again won first prize at the Leamington Music Festival while the full Choir gained a creditable second place in the village churches section. The following year, however, Styles resigned to become organist and choirmaster at Hampton Lucy. Three Choirmasters followed in fairly quick succession and the Choir's earlier achievements were never repeated.

St Laurence's Sunday School, 1958 St Laurence Church Collection

Sunday Schools provided another important link between the church and the community. From the late nineteenth until the mid- twentieth century both the Methodist chapel and the Parish Church had flourishing Sunday Schools. One of the attractions of

Sunday School was the annual outing, a rare opportunity for some children to travel beyond their own neighbourhood. These outings ceased during the war, resuming, in the case of the Parish Church, in August 1946 with a visit to Weston-super-Mare. In later years Sutton Park became a favourite destination, as was Wicksteed Park near Kettering. The Parish Magazine described how, on arrival at Wicksteed in August 1955, the children were given instructions as to 'time for tea' and where to assemble:

> *Within two minutes there was not a child to be seen – they simply vanished*
> *to the various amusement places they remembered from their previous*
> *visits, and how they revelled in it all.*

Surprisingly, there was only one 'anxious incident' when a small girl fell into the water and was pretty badly soaked, but she was attended to by the Park staff on duty.

The Church bells played an important part in the life of the village, not only ringing for local celebrations but also to mark national events. Since their installation in 1791 six bells served the community without interruption until the outbreak of the Second World War when all church bells were only to be rung if invasion was thought imminent. Ringing resumed in 1942 when the threat had passed. When Frank Spiers first learned to ring at the age of 12, ringers were often recruited from the choir:

> *When we boys were in the Choir some of us would put our cassocks on and*
> *go and watch the bell ringers for service. One Sunday Arthur Shorey, the*
> *Ringing Master, asked four of us big boys if we would like to learn to ring.*

Bidford Bellringers, 1958 St Laurence Church Collection
L to R: Frank Spiers, Fred Spiers, Sid Reade, Pam Easthope, Mary Moore, n/k, Arthur Shorey, Donald Busby, Rev Moxon, Elizabeth Moore, Jack Moore, Derek Hall, Alan Moore.

A serious problem arose in August 1953 when, according to the Bidford Bellringers Log, 'the Bells in this Tower were found to be unsafe for further ringing…and an appeal for £1,500 was launched'. The Rev Harrison, in the March edition of the Parish Magazine, appealed to all parishioners to help with the fund-raising since the bells 'belong to the village'. In less than six months the total was reached. Mr S G

Faire and his son donated a bell in memory of the late Mrs Faire, and the Barrons Bell Trust funded a second new bell. The old and new bells were dedicated on 21 December 1954 by the Bishop of Coventry.

'An appetite for entertainment'

Bidford boasted a variety of societies and organisations that catered for people's 'time off'. By the 1930s Bidford had its own branch of the Women's Institute. Peggy Griffiths was a member of the WI choir which its conductor, the redoubtable Jack Styles, successfully entered in the Leamington Music Festival. The choir continued into the post-war period before being wound up. A Debating Society, formed a few years after Peggy's arrival in Bidford in 1932, 'flourished for quite a long time', meetings being held once a week in an upstairs room in The Mason's Arms.

A film presentation company gave a movie show every Saturday in the Assembly Rooms. Audiences were large enough to warrant two performances, and the shows only came to an end when the wooden floors and staircase were declared a fire hazard. One of the highlights of the year was a visit to the Jubilee Hall by the travelling Dramatic Company, The Lauderdales, who stayed for a week and, according to Peggy Griffiths, performed some 'quite bloodcurdling shows' much enjoyed by the large audiences.

In 1936, aware of the local appetite for entertainment, Peggy started her own Concert Party, The Revellers, which was recruited entirely from the village. The first members, aged between eight and 12, were Marjorie Crompton (later Kidson), Betty Orme, Joan Griffiths and Dorrie Clarke, who learned tap and soft shoe dancing and popular songs. Adult members included singers and dancers and the comedian Arthur 'Yampy' Tedd. Dorothy Johnson remembers Tedd as 'the one that used to dress up as a bride and sing "There was I Waiting at the Church"'. Peggy's mother made all the costumes: 'Pierrots in black and yellow with tartan ruffles, skull caps, pom-poms, beauty patches and all'. The first public performance, in aid of Hockey Club funds, took place in the Jubilee Hall to a packed audience and The Revellers were soon putting on regular monthly concerts to assist other local organisations. During the war they visited several local Army Camps and the Officers' Mess at Long Marston and continued performing for several years in peacetime before disbanding.

A prerequisite for these public concerts, film shows and dramatic productions was the availability of suitable venues. When the Jubilee Hall was demolished after the war and the Assembly Rooms no longer deemed safe for such events, the village found itself

**THE CRAWFORD MEMORIAL HALL
AND SOCIAL CENTRE**

At a Public Meeting called by the Bidford-on-Avon Parish Council, at the Co-operative Hall on Wednesday, November 7th, 1945, the following resolution was passed unanimously:

That a Committee of ten members be formed which shall always include the Chairman and Vice-Chairman of the Parish Council then in office and eight members elected from this meeting. The Committee shall have power to raise and receive money on behalf of the fund; to examine and approve sites and plans; and to carry out the scheme to their approval.

COMMITTEE:

F. J. Adkins ....Chairman of the Parish Council
G. E. B. Richards ...Vice-Chairman
Dr. M. V. Murray...Chairman of the Committee
W. L. Moore ....} Joint Hon. Treasurers
S. G. Faire ....}
R. E. Noise ....Hon. Secretary
W. Paddock
E. Searson
G. H. Langston
G. Crompton

Co-opted Members:
Mrs. Bayne and Miss D. Bateman.

FINANCIAL STATEMENT TO DATE.

	£	s.	d.
From Crawford Memorial Fund	1210	5	4
,, Bidford National Savings Committee	650	0	0
,, Private subscriptions	322	16	0
,, Proceeds of Concerts, Dances, etc. ...	480	6	7
Grand Total	£2663	7	11

The Committee take this opportunity of expressing their deep appreciation of the efforts of all who have assisted, to date, in their efforts to raise funds.

1.

without adequate provision. However, in 1945 a Committee was formed to raise funds for a Community Hall to honour the memory of Dr Crawford who had died in 1943. The outcome was the Crawford Memorial Hall which, since its opening in 1955, has remained the principal venue for social functions and entertainment in the village. Provision was further enhanced by two other developments. From the late forties onwards the Hall of the Secondary School was regularly used as a venue for dramatic productions, concerts and a variety of community functions including the Old Folks' Party. Moreover, when the Infant School transferred to new school buildings in Victoria Road in 1950, the Old Schoolroom was designated, according to the Parish Magazine, to become, 'a furnished Church Hall for meetings and social gatherings' available to the whole community.

Old Folks' Party, c1960 © Evesham Journal

Menu

The trouble with being a parent is that by the time you are experienced you're unemployed

———

Roast Turkey
Bread Sauce   Stuffing
Roast Pork
Bread Rolls   Sausage
Roast and Creamed Potatoes
Green Peas and Sprouts

———

A friend is the first person who comes in when the world goes out

———

Christmas Pudding
Brandy Sauce

———

The time comes for every woman to stop patting herself on the back and start patting herself on the chin

———

Celery, Cheese and Biscuits

———

What a pity it is that nobody knows how to manage a wife except a bachelor

———

Coffee

Programme

True eloquence consists in saying all that is necessary and nothing but what is necessary

———

OFFICIAL WELCOME BY THE CHAIRMAN

———

When singleness is bliss, it's folly to be wives

———

During the evening the entertainment
will be provided by
DICK BRIGHT'S CONCERT PARTY

———

Wild oats will get sown some time, and one of the arts of life is to sow them at the right time

———

Mince Tarts and Coffee

———

It is always the best to speak the truth unless, of course, you are an exceptional liar

———

Auld Lang Syne

———

The Queen

———

FAREWELL at approximately 10.30 p.m.

Old Folks' Party, 1962 Rodney Crompton Collection

'Shall we dance?'

During the first half of the last century dancing was regarded as a desirable social accomplishment. Frank Spiers and Norah Hiatt attended the dances held at the Jubilee Hall in the thirties, and Betty Harris and Rodney Crompton remember attending dances at the Assembly Rooms after the war before they were deemed unsafe for such use. After the war Bill Churchley's dance band appeared regularly in the village, with Bill on drums, Jack Treadgold on piano and Peter Churchley, who also sang, on accordion. Peter Warwick recalls that they had a good reputation.

TUESDAY, APRIL 23rd, 1946.
Jubilee Hall

THE COMMITTEE'S
BIG
DANCE
8 p.m. — 1 a.m.
: *FEASEY'S DANCE BAND* :
TICKETS:
12s. 6d. Double : 7s. 6d. Single
Including Refreshments.

For young men and young women dances provided excellent opportunities for meeting. Not all parents, however, were happy for their daughters to frequent such unregulated environments. When asked by her future husband Frank, 'There's a dance on up at Welford, would you like to come?' Ivy Webb replied, 'Oh, I would but my Mom and Dad would never allow me to go to a dance'. Obviously keen to accept the date, Ivy said to her friend: 'Nancy, I wonder if they would let me go if you was to tell a bit of a lie and say you're coming with me'. Nancy agreed and with this assurance Ivy's parents gave their permission, though not without conditions: 'Provided I fetch you home, and you come home at 10 o'clock', insisted her father.

Morris dancing in Bidford had a long history but during the nineteenth century the tradition had largely died out. In 1886 D'Arcy Ferris, a musical entrepreneur from Cheltenham, revived the Bidford Morris. Ferris took his new team on a commercial tour through the Cotswolds and Shakespeare country, attracting large crowds.

Bidford's most significant musician of the time was violinist and shoe-maker John Robbins. Aware that the pipe and tabor were traditional to the Morris, Ferris sent Robbins to study with Ilmington Morris' piper James John Arthur. On a wave of national interest, Cecil Sharp published Robbins' performances in the first volume of 'The Morris Book' in 1907, as traditional Bidford Morris tunes. Their local authenticity remains a matter of some dispute, but 'Shepherd's Hey' was arranged by several composers, notably Percy Grainger. The Shakespeare Bidford Morris Dancers, as they were called, continued until membership was depleted by the war of 1914-18. Jack Robbins trained and conducted a Bidford drum and fife band, and, in 1903, a small local orchestra comprising strings, brass and woodwind, which became very popular. He died in Bidford in 1948.

In 1955 a new team of young boys was formed under the leadership of John Masterson. It performed until 1964 at various village occasions including the annual Carnival. In 1969 the Shakespeare Morris Men from Stratford revived Ferris' Bidford dances and reintroduced the tradition of dancing in the village square on Trinity Monday and during the August Carnival.

The Sporting Life

For those with a sporting inclination Bidford offered an increasing range of possibilities. Two sports that gained in popularity after the Second World War were hockey and tennis. In 1957 the Hockey Club's application for a playing pitch on the Big Meadow was accepted by the Parish Council, even though their request the following March for permission to build a pavilion was turned down. The first tennis courts were sited behind the Reliance Garage, but they fell into disrepair during the war and were relocated as part of the Crawford Hall development in the 1950s. The Tennis Club attracted an increasing number of young people, according to Peter Warwick, and continued to flourish in subsequent decades.

Bidford Tennis Club, c1960 © Stratford Herald
Back Row L to R: Winnie Holman, n/k, Phil Jones, Don Mayrick, Chris Williams.
Front Row L to R: Dot Collett, Val Hamblin, Joy Mayrick, Josie Holt, Shelagh Murray.

Nevertheless, football and cricket, already popular by the beginning of the century, remained the dominant sports throughout the period. As a child in the 1920s, Frank Spiers remembers hearing stories of how the Bidford football team used to go by horse and cart to play at places like Badsey, Bretforton and the Littletons with plenty of homemade wine on board, returning to Bidford around eight o'clock with the oil lamps lit on the cart, and the bottles presumably empty.

Bidford Football Team, 1950s (Audrie Spiers Collection)
Back Row L to R: Mr Gowers, Len Hartwell, Les Smith, Wilf Busby, Harold Taylor.
Middle Row L to R: Frank Spiers, Don Mayrick, Les Gould, Jim Vincent, Tom Cole,
Harold Bennett, Reg Beard.
Front Row L to R: Gordon Lock, Ernie Bennett, Alan Radbourn, Geoff Clee, Bill Beard.

The football ground before the war was in a meadow on the Barton side of the bridge, but after the war it moved to the Big Meadow. During the immediate post-war period and throughout the 1950s, Bidford had one of the strongest sides in the Stratford League. The 1948/9 season was one of Bidford's most successful. The team won the League and the Stratford Nursing Home Cup and reached the final of the Stratford Hospital Cup only to lose to Littleton. For two years the team's outside-right was the local Methodist minister, the Rev Arthur Hoof. The coach, manager and organiser of the football club in these years was Wilf 'Cloggy' Busby, so nicknamed, according to Mike Paddock, because his simple approach to the opposition was 'kick him, or knock him out'. The appeal of football extended well beyond the football club. Mike Paddock recalls:

If we had a spare hour we'd go out (to the fields) and play…you picked two teams and you played the match over the week. It didn't matter about the score, we just kept playing.

Mike's other sporting obsession was cricket. He started playing aged 12 when the cricket ground was situated in a field in Grange Road where the gymkhanas were held. Cricket was scarcely less popular than football. The Cricket Club ran two teams, and soon after the move to the Big Meadow, Mike helped to build the first pavilion and to raise money for the third pavilion, which stands today.

Several interviewees commented on how male sport in particular played an essential part in bringing together people of different social backgrounds. At the very least it served as a 'mixing pot' if not a 'melting pot' of class distinctions. Amongst those of acknowledged status in Bidford who were enthusiastic sportsmen, Rodney Crompton's father George, the owner of the Reliance Garage and a Rural District Councillor, and Dr Michael Murray, the local GP, were for many years members of the village hockey team, whilst several of the bigger farmers played in the cricket team alongside their employees and other working men from the village.

Whether played by children in the streets and fields or in teams organised by school or club, sport further highlighted the outdoor and communal nature of many of Bidford's leisure activities during the early and middle decades of the last century.

Chapter 6

BIDFORD AT WAR

When the twentieth century dawned, a now largely forgotten conflict, the Boer War, was at its height. Victorian Britain was a deeply patriotic nation and the war brought that sense of national pride to the fore. In March 1900, when news of the relief of the Siege of Ladysmith was received in Bidford, the report in the Evesham Journal spoke of:

> ...great rejoicing. Numbers of flags were soon flying, including the Union Jack upon the church tower. The bells rang forth merrily in the evening and in the usual Bidford fashion the event was celebrated by a dinner at the White Lion hotel.

There were 21 men from Bidford on active service during the Boer War. The Parish Magazine for March 1900 records that the £12 raised from a concert at the White Lion Hotel 'has been spent on providing comforts for these men, and the ladies of the parish…have sent them woollen helmets and other articles for their use which we trust will prove of great value'. They clearly were, as the June Magazine published letters received from grateful Bidford soldiers. The Boer War, however, was to pale into insignificance compared to the two wars that Britain faced in the first half of the new century.

1914: 'All over Europe the Lamps are going out'

Bidford men were among the first recruits in 1914. At least 24 young men volunteered in the first few weeks of the war. Many more joined up in the years that followed, especially after conscription was introduced in January 1916.

58 Bidford men lost their lives in 'the Great War'. Such losses would have had a profound effect on a population of just over 1,400. Harry Freeman's story is particularly tragic. He was in the police force in Sutton Coldfield and came home during time off only to find his fiancée outside the Bull's Head with another man. An argument followed during which Harry took the engagement ring from her finger and threw it in the road! He then travelled straight to Worcester to enlist in the Worcestershire Regiment. He

Col Ludlow appealing for recruits Rodney Crompton collection

was killed the following year in Belgium when a shell exploded in his trench. There was no body and his name is commemorated on the Menin Gate at Ypres.

Most of those who died were farm labourers and shop workers who had never been further than Stratford. The village supported the war effort, showing a grim determination to support their boys as illustrated in War Weapon Week, 11-17 August 1918. The Evesham Journal reported:

> *An open air meeting was held on Sunday evening on the Bank…There was a large attendance, Mr Sam Mason presided…and Mr H. C. Lacey (hon. organising secretary) delivered a stirring address.*

Bidford was asked to invest £4,000 for the purchase of four guns, the cost of the first gun having already been promised. The Rev J W Evans' resolution pledging the meeting to do all in their power to exceed the target figure 'was carried by acclamation', according to the Evesham Journal, and an office under the Assembly Rooms for the receipt of investments was placed at the disposal of the committee during Gun Week. During the week:

> *Concerts were held on the Pleasure Grounds. A very excellent and miscellaneous programme was arranged by Mr A. W. Warner the artistes*

For our boys © Warwickshire County Council PH352/30/42

being "Warner's Pink Pierrots". Friday was the children's day, the scholars from each school marched in procession from their schools to the War Savings office and made their investments. All the children... then proceeded to Holland's Pleasure Grounds where an excellent tea was provided….Trips on the steamers on the Avon then followed, then games were entered into with zest.

Each child was given 6d and a similar amount was placed 'to their credit' in the War Savings Association, a scheme for raising money for the war effort which became widespread from 1916 onwards. By the end of the week, £10,584 had been raised. This was an impressive sum of money for a small community, the vast majority of whom were poorly paid labourers and artisans. Their determination to 'do their bit' was fuelled by the tragic losses of loved ones involved in the conflict. A month after Gun Week, the Evesham Journal was reporting the death of another Bidford soldier:

Mrs E. Russell of Tower Hill has received official information that her youngest son, Pte Reginald Russell of the Royal Warwickshire Regiment, was killed in action in France on August 21st. He was 20 years of age…The eldest son of Mrs Russell was killed in France about two years ago.

The same newspaper spoke of the village's intense relief and joy at the ending of the war in November 1918:

> *Upon receipt of the splendid news there was an outburst of enthusiasm and in a very short time flags of almost all sizes and designs were flying from homes. Work ceased and everyone seemed bent on celebrating the joyful event. At 8 o'clock in the evening a huge bonfire was lighted on Tower Hill in the presence of a large enthusiastic assembly who sang and cheered themselves hoarse as they watched the flames. Quite a number of houses were illuminated and the bells pealed forth merrily from the church tower.*

The War Memorial. Rodney Crompton Collection

On 29 April 1923 a War Memorial was erected in the village square. Local stone mason, Fred Houghton, made the stone cross. Frank Spiers remembers growing up during the thirties in a village where there was more than the usual number of widows. On Armistice Day the church was full of bereaved families whose loved ones' names were on the memorial. In 1939 the country found itself at war again, a war that would see more names added to those who had died in the 'war to end all wars'.

'The Long-dreaded day has arrived'

Rodney Crompton remembers standing outside Bloodworth's bakery with his mother in the spring of 1939:

> *...there was an Easter egg in the window, shaped like a horse and cart with a load of hay on it and with little yellow chickens. She said, 'Have a good look at that because you won't see anything like this again for a long time'.*

Describing Hitler as 'the supreme example of GODLESSNESS', the Vicar referred to the outbreak of war in the October Parish Magazine: 'The long-dreaded day has arrived, and Europe has once more been plunged into war'. Evensong was brought forward to 3.30 pm as the blackout took effect, there was no afternoon Sunday School and no midnight communion on Christmas Eve. The December Magazine announced that:

> *A committee has been formed...to collect money and inaugurate efforts to enable Bidford to send to the men from this parish serving with the forces... parcels or gifts from time to time to let them see they are not forgotten.*

In August 1940 the Magazine noted that ' more and more men from Bidford are joining HM Forces', leaving relatives in fear of the dreaded telegram. In September there was news that Privates Smith and Pulham, who were reported 'missing', were alive but had been taken prisoner. In May 1943 Mr and Mrs Bryan heard that their son Harry, who had been reported as 'missing', was now confirmed as 'killed in action'. Frank Spiers remembered Harry as a clever lad who had passed the eleven-plus exam and had gone to Alcester Grammar School. Frank had Harry's motor bike after he was killed. There was still no news of District Nurse Thomas' pilot husband who had been 'missing' for some time. He was later confirmed as 'killed in action'.

Others however did return including Douglas Bott who, the Magazine recorded in 1943,

> *...was wounded at Dunkirk in the early days of the war and has been a prisoner in Germany for three and a half years...We sympathise with him for the loss of a foot, but are thankful that...he will be able to be fitted up with an artificial limb....It is wonderful to see him overcoming his disability in the way he does, and the other night he was enjoying playing ping-pong and billiards [in the Boys' Club] without the aid of his crutch.*

For some, the war was fought thousands of miles from home. A touching letter to his mother from 'one of our boys serving in India' was featured in the Parish Magazine for June 1943:

> *The time is now 10.30 pm. I have just got back from the Pictures. Now of all things, they showed a short supporting picture of Shakespeare's county and, of all places, Bidford-on-Avon. Just imagine, thousands of miles away from home in a very remote part of India, in a tiny picture house, they show my own village! My heart turned over when I saw the very familiar church and the rooftops.*

The Home Front

Farm produce from rural communities such as Bidford became essential in helping to feed the country. Mike Paddock remembers helping with work on his father's farm where they had poultry producing the precious eggs so carefully rationed. Providing food for a nation at war meant that farms were always working under pressure. Mike recalled:

> *We never had a holiday. I went to my sister's on the Bank Holiday to help with the harvest there for six weeks and that was when everything was done by hand and they went round with a tractor, stacked the sheaves up and threw them on top of a wagon.*

Much of the work had to be done by women. Betty Harris remembers her mother and other women 'working in the fields pea-picking, plum-picking around where we lived. A lot of them didn't have husbands at home'.

Living in a rural area, however, did have its advantages according to Mike Paddock:

> *Really and honestly we were never affected by the rationing. Like everyone else we did a bit of bartering. A dozen eggs for some bacon or a side of ham or beef. We used to have sugar by the half hundredweight. We had our own petrol tank during the war as well [and] used red diesel for the lorries as well as the tractors.*

Rodney Crompton commented:

> *I don't think the war years did us any harm because we had a very good diet...We got all the fruit and vegetables plus eggs from this area. We had it a lot easier out in the country.*

Despite being well fed, there were no luxuries and Rodney remembers shopping at the Co-op in Bidford:

I remember that my mother's Co-op number was 50. You always had your number when you went shopping. [However], Philip Tyas' father was in India and sent a coconut back. I remember it being delivered in a cardboard box. We drilled a hole and we all had a small cup of juice. That was the first exotic fruit I had ever seen.

Help on many local farms came with POWs who were assigned to agricultural work. Gerhard Schober came to the area after his capture in Le Havre in 1944. He had been in the German navy and was nineteen when he was captured and ended up in Honeybourne. In his experience, local people didn't resent POWs:

I worked doing apple picking and pea-picking. We worked the same hours as the ordinary workers. Sometimes we had to work overtime…We lived in huts. We did our own cooking and we went to the village shop to get the bread rations we were entitled to. There were ten of us. We got a ration book which was left at the shop and the firm paid for whatever we bought. Once we were working on the farm, you were allowed to go so many miles and that was it. Birmingham…was too far.

Other workers were land army girls, one of whom later became his wife.

Betty Harris remembers seeing POWs working in the fields round the village: 'They all went round with these great big patches on them so you knew who they were…and they would cycle up the village and go in the fields'. According to Rodney Crompton, people 'certainly preferred to have German POWs to Italians. The Germans worked and the Italians were useless! …The POWs were a curiosity for us kids'.

The Defence of the Realm

Bidford wanted to 'do its bit' for the war effort and at the beginning of the war all the railings from the houses along the High Street were removed in the campaign to collect as much metal as possible to help make aircraft.

Those men who had not been called up joined the Bidford Home Guard. Frank Spiers acted as a messenger boy:

It was like 'Dad's Army'. It was all the old soldiers and people that were in factory jobs or weren't fit enough to go in the army…Us boys were messenger boys, and the squad [was based] in the old house in Waterloo Road…where the platoon slept at night. But we slept at the Police Station in a cell, with old Bill Munday the policeman…I would go on duty at

10 pm and sleep in the cell and if any messages came, he would take them and I'd have to run up to the platoon at Waterloo Road. And then we'd come off duty at 6 am. I'd probably have something to eat and change from my uniform into my work clothes and then at 6.30 am I'd cycle off to work in Redditch.

Bidford Cadet force Frank Spiers Collection

Frank recalls training being quite rigorous. On Wednesdays, 'we all met in the High School where regular officers and a sergeant from the army would come and teach us about guns, ammunition, tactics and grenades'. They were also taken to Kineton to be trained in how to throw hand grenades and use rifles. Every Sunday they paraded in their uniforms and had to do drill exercises. Frank enjoyed the sporting opportunities provided by the Home Guard:

I can remember the Battalion having a sports day at Ragley Park. 100 people walked from Bidford as there was no petrol for motoring. I was 17 and came second in the mile race. We played a lot of friendly [soccer] matches against army teams from Long Marston, Kineton and RAF teams from Honeybourne and Defford. Some had professional players. We had a mixed team of some 17 year olds and older men exempt from going in the forces.

In Rodney Crompton's view, the Home Guard:

...used to have a whale of a time, rushing up and down the High Street flinging bangers. We used to go off to choir practice and there they were with their rifles. But then, you see, they were all we'd got, and if it had ever come to pass I'm sure we would have needed them.

As in 'Dad's Army', the village had its air-raid wardens and Rodney's father was one of them: 'As far as I can see they went down to their meeting places and played cards and drank! They would go and check to see if all the blackout curtains were up'.

Warwickshire County Council.

L. EDGAR STEPHENS,
CLERK OF THE COUNTY
COUNCIL.

TELEGRAMS:- STEPHENS, WARWICK.
TELEPHONE Nº 371. (3 LINES).

IN REPLY
PLEASE   JCT/NK.
QUOTE ....

YOUR REF. ....

OFFICE OF THE CLERK OF THE COUNCIL,

SHIRE HALL,

WARWICK.

11th. January, 1938.

Dear Sir,

AIR DEFENCE.

Referring to our previous correspondence in this matter, your letter of the 21st. idem was submitted to a meeting of the Small Holdings Committee held yesterday.

The Committee are prepared to permit an observer post to be established on Burrow Hill Small Holding, Bidford-on-Avon in the manner indicated in your letter, provided that, in the event of any damage being occasioned thereby, suitable compensation or reinstatement will be made to the Council or their tenant.

Yours faithfully,

Clerk of the Council.

The Northern Area Commandant,
    Observer Corps.
        R.A.F. Station,
        Hucknall,
        NOTTS.

113

Other Bidford men belonged to the Royal Observer Corps whose vital work was done at their post at the top of Tower Hill. Peggy Griffiths and her husband Jack ran the Post Office and she recalls how in 1937 strangers visited Jack to inform him that an observer post was being installed in the area and he was to be the chief observer and was to recruit 12-14 trustworthy men to maintain it. From 1939 the post was manned day and night. Jack would spend the day there and be home at 6 pm for some sleep before taking over the manual telephone exchange at 10 pm. When there was an alert, and that was frequently, he knew there would be no sleep on the camp bed by the telephone exchange until the 'all clear' had sounded. He had to alert the police, fire stations and all the local services. Some nights when Coventry was under attack, the alert lasted for hours. Peggy was sure that Jack did not have an unbroken night's sleep for six years

Jack Griffiths 'at war'
By kind permission of Brewin Books

Betty Harris' father, Cyril Smith, joined the Observer Corps in 1939. He had wanted to join the RAF but was rejected because he had a heart problem. As a little girl during the war, Betty had the job of taking her father's dinner up to him when he was on duty: 'But we couldn't take it up to the post because that was top secret. They used to say "Friend or foe?" Well you can imagine, can't you, when they said "Friend or foe?", I thought they were going to shoot me!' She would wait for one of the Observer Corps to come and collect her father's dinner from her. According to Frank Spiers, the Observer Corps 'would be up there all night identifying aircraft flying over and phoning through to anti-aircraft batteries to tell them what aircraft were heading their way'. Betty Harris claimed that many of the Observer Corps were so good that they could recognise a plane from the noise even when some distance away.

Very few bombs were dropped. Rodney Crompton remembers that when one fell at Barton, 'we all stood round and looked at the hole. There was another one dropped by the bridge at Broom and you can still see the crater in the river bank'. Nevertheless, aircraft flew over Bidford regularly and Betty Harris remembers her grandmother, who lived in Grafton Lane, saying that one night it was so bad that all the residents came out of their council houses and hid under a hedge. For a small child like Betty, war was a frightening experience:

> *…it was very dark in those days. I mean, we had all the blinds down and no lights. Older people…didn't realise that children were listening to them talk and you used to have nightmares about the Germans. There were four cottages where we lived and one cellar. When the siren went we all went down there.*

Air-raids during school hours, however, were a welcome break for Rodney Crompton. When the air-raid siren sounded, 'we used to say, "Thanks Jerry"'. There was a procedure which all the children knew:

> *When the air-raid siren went the teacher used to open the door and stand back. We were gone like rabbits. We all had a house to go to. I used to go down Grange Road to the last house on the left and by the time I got there the door was open. Straight under the dining room table. I remember it had a cloth with a fringe all around the bottom. I shot straight under there and after about two minutes a hand would appear with a glass of milk and a biscuit. Then the 'all clear' went and we said, 'Thanks very much', and went back to school.*

He also remembered being given a gas mask:

> *You carried them everywhere; if you didn't, you were in trouble. They were terrible things. We had to wear them in class one day. They got steamed up when you breathed and they were smelly.*

One raid that was indelibly etched in the memories was the Coventry blitz on 14 November 1940. Rodney recalls:

> *We stood in the back garden and we could see the flames. It was all blacked out so a fire that size, even 20 miles away, showed up well; the sky was bright red.*

For Betty Harris, 'that was a big night. I can remember all the people from Tower Hill were outside and we were watching Coventry burn. It was quite frightening really'. As a young boy Mike Paddock remembers being on a lorry delivering produce to the wholesale market in Coventry during the Blitz: 'It was just heaps of rubble everywhere'.

There was an aerodrome at Honeybourne where Lancaster bomber crews were based. Rodney Crompton's father used to meet a gang of them at the White Lion Hotel:

> *…and sometimes bring them home, and mother used to get ham and eggs for them or fish and chips as we could get a certain amount of illicit food. Every now and then one didn't come back… They used to say, 'so-and-so*

is missing'...I think they lost two or three. We'd stand on the back lawn in the evening and see the planes coming over from all parts, and they would go round in a big circle, so all these streams of light would come from different airfields and merge and all go off in the same direction...

Sometimes, 'you used to get low flying planes. In those days low flying meant 100 foot...You could see the pilot's eyes when they went over'.

Since Bidford Bridge was a vital crossing point, 'there was a big 14 lb gun', Rodney Crompton recalled, 'mounted on a massive concrete block where the Bridge Restaurant is now, and a machine gun post in a pillbox on the other side of the bridge'. Mike Paddock's brother was in the Home Guard. They were given instructions that if any enemy tanks came over the bridge they were to try and stop them. They were told: 'Make sure you get them with the first shot because the building will collapse otherwise'.

In keeping with other rural communities Bidford took in evacuees from Birmingham and Coventry. Betty Harris' family:

...had an evacuee from Birmingham called June Hammond. She was with us for about two or three years. I wasn't very old, I remember her coming and telling me there wasn't a Father Christmas! I remember her father being in the RAF and he came down with her mother to stay occasionally. Next door, Mrs Freeman's niece used to come and bring her boys. Her husband worked in a factory in Birmingham. Her son Pete was an evacuee and went to school with me right up until the end of the war.

Mary Paddock's 'Granny' Holder also had evacuees and her abiding impression of them was that 'their heads were full of lice'. Rodney Crompton noted that some of the evacuees could not cope with country life and returned to Birmingham or Coventry despite the danger. Otherwise, they 'just slotted in with the village kids'.

The Beginning of the End

After the Americans entered the war in December 1941, they took over the airfield at Long Marston the following year and soon made their presence felt in Bidford. According to Mike Paddock:

Most of the stonework on top of the bridge isn't old because when the Americans came...with tank transporters they would knock the wall down. How the tank transporters got round what was the White Lion Hotel I don't know!

Rodney Crompton remembers: 'We used to try their chewing gum. You'd see them walking round the High Street. There was a military hospital at the bottom of Grange

Road at Avonside and we'd see them walking around in their blue uniforms'. Frank Spiers talks of how the Americans and other servicemen from bases round the area would cycle into Bidford, drink in all the pubs and also go to the dances held at the Jubilee Hall. With so many servicemen at the dances 'us youngsters couldn't get a dance, so we had lessons from Doreen Clark at Bell Court'.

The American base had a special visitor in 1943. Joe Louis, the world heavyweight champion, came to the base for a fight. Frank Spiers was a keen amateur boxer and was thrilled when the local GP, Dr Murray (who had a car) took Frank with him up to the base to watch the fight.

June 1944 saw the tide of the war turn with the D-Day invasion. The July Parish Magazine called for all in Bidford to pray for 'our splendid men who have landed on the beaches and are pushing their way through the enemy'. Beginning on the evening of D-Day there was a gathering in the church each Wednesday at 7 pm for 15 minutes of prayer, 'and it has been very encouraging to see so many of our people present'. As the tide of the war turned, the Home Guard received orders to stand down and the December Magazine expressed its gratitude to the Bidford Home Guard 'for all the time they have put in'. The blackout was relaxed enabling Evensong to revert to 6.30 pm and Midnight Eucharist to be held on Christmas Eve.

The end of the war in Europe was greeted with rejoicing in Bidford. Betty Harris' mother took her down to the Bull's Head pub 'where they were burning an effigy of Hitler. They had a great big bonfire and a party at the Bull's Head. We had a party up on Tower Hill. Everybody was so happy'. Thanksgiving services were held at Broom and Bidford on VE Day and on the following Sunday. The Parish Magazine captured the atmosphere:

> *The ringing of the bells, the racing and dancing in the High Street, the huge bonfire with its effigy stuck in the centre, the fireworks, the coloured flares and the various tea parties that were arranged…for the youngsters.*
> *The Memorial too was splendidly floodlit and was an outstanding reminder of the price of war and the sacrifice the men of the last campaign paid.*

Chapter 7

REFLECTIONS

Bidford emerged from the Second World War as a close-knit community well served by rail and road links, a wide range of High Street shops, an established Junior and Infant School and, since 1938, a Secondary School with a growing reputation. During the next 40 years, however, the village was transformed. There were positive developments – provision of main drainage in the early 1960s and the creation of a stock of affordable (Council) housing over the following 15 years being two of the most important – but the loss of the railway by 1962, the secondary school in 1985 and the High Street shops from the sixties onwards were a succession of body blows to the life of the village.

Bidford sidings, 1949 © Roger Carpenter

As a local businessman, Mike Paddock was aware of the value of the rail links to the main industrial and commercial centres in the Midlands and further afield during the forties and fifties:

> *[We put] potatoes on the train at Bidford Siding and at Broom. The amount of coal we shifted on the trucks [for the Co-op] is nobody's business… There were a terrific amount of trains, I'm sure they had iron ore on, …*

going down to Wales. They'd come up to Broom Junction and then down towards Ashchurch. Twelve months before they closed the railway through here they closed the whole thing off, reballasted it and put down brand new lines all the way from Stratford…then the next year they closed it! It never makes sense when you think about it. Why close all the railways, because they were used tremendously for freight?

And Bidford was only a halt on a minor cross-country route.

Many locals thought of the railway simply in terms of shopping trips to Redditch and Birmingham, or awayday excursions to seaside resorts. Very few of those interviewed seemed to regret its loss, or even remember it. An exception to this is Ivy Webb, who did war work on the railway at Broom:

I had to get a job, but I tried not to go away into the forces. I went on the railway at Broom in the signal box…We had to work shifts… there was no specific training as such, you just sort of picked it up from the person as was doing it, pulling levers.

A replica of Broom station, complete with island platform, but without Ivy's signal box, can be seen at the Midland Railway Centre at Swanwick in Derbyshire. By 2011 the Honeybourne line had been rebuilt, and there was talk of reopening the Stratford – Cheltenham rail link.

The first Bidford High School minibus Brian Cobb Collection
L to R: Rodney Crompton, Harry Smith PTA, Joy Mayrick, Joan Huckfield, Brian Banting Chair of Governors, Ray Stanley PTA, Alan Hunt Headmaster, Brian Cobb, the Head Girl and Head Boy with their deputies.

For most interviewees, the event that seemed to arouse the most powerful upsurge of anger among villagers was the transfer of the Secondary School to Alcester. Founded in 1938, the School prospered during the Second World War. It was a popular and successful school, both academically and as a focal point for social events, but from the late 1960s onwards its catchment was reduced progressively to facilitate the concentration of local secondary education in Alcester. This not only limited the number of pupils it could take, but also defined the curriculum range and the number of teaching staff in terms of the mandatory pupil/teacher ratios in operation at the time.

Brian Cobb joined the School Staff in 1973 as Head of Geography, and was Head of Upper School when it was shut down in 1985. He organized the further education programme, and worked with the Parents' Association throughout his stay. He explained that the school swimming pool, the money for which had been raised by public subscription, was never used as a community facility because it was a learner pool, and

> ...there were difficulties about public use and health and safety considerations. Warwickshire County Council had it tightly under their control, and the teaching staff avoided it.

The County Council seemed to be squeezing the life out of the School before it was eventually shut down, and the land sold for housing development. In the opinion of Les Smith (who had been the building foreman at the School):

> The Council made a lot of mistakes. They knocked that school down just to get a few thousand pounds...and they haven't got the playing field they had before.

The problem was that the land and everything built on it belonged in law to the County Council, who were free to do what they wished with it. Any capital receipts it yielded could be used to support developments elsewhere in the County. Brian Slaughter, who was a Governor of the School, a parent, and the County Councillor for Bidford at the time, was heavily criticized locally for a sequence of events over which he personally had very little control.

Reflections on their schooldays during the seventies and eighties were given by more than 20 ex-pupils and all their memories were happy ones. Quite apart from its achievements academically, the School provided a focus for community activities such as parties, dances and Christmas pantomimes. As Jill Houghton recalls:

> Every year at Christmas an event was put on in the hall: a full blown production or a musical such as 'Oliver' and the whole of the village paid to see it.

How much the School was appreciated by its pupils is apparent from two of her later comments: first, that while the School was still open, its grounds were a favourite evening meeting place for young teenagers in the summer; and second, that in later years, pupil reunions of all kinds have always been a tremendous success. In its day Bidford High School was also home to local adult education, and when it closed a range of practical learning opportunities for all age groups in the community was lost.

There is no doubt of the cost to village amenity resulting from loss of the School, but there has at least been one recent compensation. The playing field referred to by Mr Smith, which lies at the far end of Dugdale Avenue, has come into the ownership of the Parish Council, and is now available for leisure purposes, notably junior football.

The demise of the postwar High Street is a sad story. Norah Hiatt put her finger on one major contributory factor, that in many homes before 1970, 'you hadn't got pantries, a fridge, washing machine or anything'. People's shopping habits, before freezers, microwave ovens and more sophisticated fridges became a standard feature in family houses during the 1970s were quite different from today. It was normal for housewives to shop 'little and often', and in Bidford there were several shops in every category available to do business with them. The closure of the Fisherman's Rest, Masons Arms/ Anglo-Saxon and White Lion pubs during the following 10 years had an adverse impact on High Street activity, but it was the departure of the Co-op in 1978 that proved to be decisive. The High Street was redeveloped to provide some additional amenity, notably the Health Centre, the public toilets and the area around the War Memorial, but many of the commercial premises were sold for residential occupation or small scale retail use. By 1982, the northern side of the street (including Saxonfields) had been effectively redeveloped as housing, thus making it impossible for the High Street to revert to its traditional function as a shopping centre.

The question of whether the redevelopment matched local aspirations has remained unanswered. Similarly, it is not clear whether, apart from the new houses provided, any new public benefit had been created for the village in compensation for the shops that had been lost. Whenever public opinion has been tested in recent years, there has been a consistent demand for a wider range of shops, and it certainly seems a shame that, by comparison with Stratford or Alcester, the present-day High Street on a Saturday afternoon is virtually deserted.

The major local controversy that divided the community in the 1970s was not the High Street as such, but the plans for construction of the relief road (B439). A body of opinion

The bypass showing the modern Fire Station Sandra Parker Collection

in the village, led by Walter Lewis, a Parish and District Councillor, who was also passionately involved in Bidford High School and its swimming pool, took the view that the sorely needed relief road should follow the former railway line from Cranhill, two miles east of Bidford, to Broom Junction. Here, it would join the new major road being built from Evesham to Stratford, and through traffic would disperse from there.

Frank Spiers was Chairman of the Parish Council, and while keen to see the chronic traffic congestion on the High Street ended, he was also anxious to keep traffic passing through the village, in order to protect the livelihood of local shops and eating places. At a strategic level, the Parish Council was also aware that neither the County Council nor the Government would tolerate the cost of building a four-mile bypass for villages on the scale of Bidford and Broom in the adverse national financial circumstances of the 1970s.

At a public meeting towards the end of 1974, Frank Spiers set out the position of the Parish Council in these terms:

> *For the last six years the Ministry…and the County Council have been trying to find a way to give relief to our narrow and congested High Street. After two public inquiries…the Inspector decided…in favour of the Inner Relief Road…We wish to give you the opportunity to express your opinions… of what we have done, and then…we shall ask you for a vote of confidence without which we do not feel that we should continue to act on your behalf.*

The Parish Council got its vote of confidence from the public.

The Department of Transport in any case had a powerful technical argument against the railway route, which concerned its effect on traffic movement on the new trunk road (A46). Its junction with the A46 would necessitate an additional roundabout on the new road midway between the A439 junction (Bidford/Harvington) and the A435 Alcester/Birmingham junction. Apart from adding to the cost of construction, the main operational consequence of opting for the railway route would be to slow traffic movement down over a five-mile stretch of road, increasing congestion and road safety risks in the process.

In this controversy, Peggy Griffiths was very definitely on the side of Mr. Lewis. She wrote:
> *I believe most of the villagers hoped it could be built on the…derelict railway track…through to Broom…which would have been ideal…We fought long and hard…but eventually we were obliged to concede ... And so at long last it materialised in late 1979.*

Barbara Mumford, who was Head Girl at Bidford High School in 1950-51, said that:
> *Mr Lewis worked very hard, and put his heart and whole life into the 'railway' route.*

Debate within the community raged hot and strong for several years and has never entirely subsided. There is still a body of opinion in Bidford which asserts that from the village point of view, the railway route was superior.

Around this time, people were becoming resigned to a series of disappointments. However, in one area of development, Bidford positively flourished during this period. House building was the growth industry. Infill housing along Waterloo Road, Victoria Road and Westholme Road was augmented by the construction of new areas feeding on to the traditional routes through and out of the village. One significant addition was Bramley Way, a new spinal road leading northwards and opening the way for further development on the far side of the B439 relief road. The total scale of these developments was such that the number of houses in the village more than doubled as the century came to an end.

Bidford's population rose from 2,800 in 1971 to 4,830 in 2001 during which period the village developed into the dormitory town prescribed in the mid-1960s structure plan, and with very little in the way of amenities for new families moving in, particularly the children and adolescents whose home it became. The Parish Council and many local people began to argue that this process should be halted, and their thoughts turned towards creating a home-grown village development plan. It was recognised that this would require an in-depth assessment of community preferences across the range of local services, out of which the reshaping of Bidford could take place. A first appraisal was attempted by Parish Councillor Angus Macdonald in 1998, and a comprehensive study of the entire parish was launched by the Council as a whole two years later.

The changes in Bidford between 1900 and 2000 were far greater than could possibly have been imagined when the young men went off to South Africa to fight in the Boer War. Yet in one way the start and finish of the century mirrored each other almost exactly. January 1901 saw major floods which left the bridge at Broom seriously damaged and many houses inundated. The Parish Magazine for February 1901 remarks that 'the sudden and disastrous flood which ended the old year upset a good many [Christmas] arrangements including the splendid treats given to the children of the parish'. Easter 1998 produced a powerful encore, but on account of the growth of the village in the meantime, many more homes and businesses were badly affected.

Floods, Easter1998 (Sandra Parker Collection)]

The weather in general was poor that year, remaining cool and wet into the first half of 1999. By this time, when people stood in the mud and the rain waiting to get into the Crawford Hall, provision of a tarmac car park became an attractive 'millennium project' for the community as it looked ahead to the twenty-first century. This time, Brian Slaughter had the last word on the subject. As Chairman of Stratford District Council in 2003, he was able to obtain the financial award that made this improvement possible.

This book is the story of 'yesterday's children': those who lived through the twentieth century, and made their own contribution to the Bidford-on-Avon of today. The last word belongs to them, as they express their wishes and hopes for Bidford during the present century:

All is not lost! There is a wonderful community spirit in the village. People have joined together to fight for the fire station and the library, and they want a voice in how the village should be run. With so many clubs and activities, there is something for everybody. Bidford was a good place to grow up in, and I hope it will remain so in the coming years.
Charles Haywood

It is time for us to hand this lovely village over to the next generations. I ask you urgently to cherish its old buildings – especially the church. Respect its traditions and keep its reputation safe as one of the friendliest villages in Warwickshire. Thank you and God bless you.
Dorothy Johnson

SELECT WRITTEN SOURCES

MANUSCRIPT SOURCES:
Bidford-on-Avon Bellringers Log Book, 1954-55
Bidford-on-Avon Parish Council: Minute Books 1950 - 1960
Murray, M *Personal Memories* (n.d.)
Warwickshire County Record Office (WRCO):
> Bidford Secondary School:
>> Admissions Register, 1939 – 1943
>> Governors' Minutes, 1938 - 1961
>> Log Book, 1938 – 1950
>> HMI Report, 1949

> **Sales Day Book,** Jesse Houghton, 1902 – 1920

PRINTED SOURCES:
> **Official sources:**
> National Census, England and Wales, 1891, 1901
> **Directories:**
> Kelly's Directory, Warwickshire, 1896, 1900, 1904, 1908, 1912, 1916, 1921, 1924, 1928, 1932, 1936, 1940
> Spennell's Annual Directory, Warwickshire, 1900, 1916
> **Newspapers and Magazines:**
> Stratford Herald
> Evesham Journal
> Bidford-on-Avon Parish Magazine:
>> 1900 – 1912 (in St Laurence Church)
>> 1932 -1956 (in WCRO)

> **Books and pamphlets:**
> Bird, V   *Warwickshire,* 1973
> Churchley, R   *Having a Drink Round Bidford, 2012*
> Comyns, B   *Sisters by a River,* 1947 (Eyre & Spottiswood), 1985 (Virago).
>   For a list of her other novels go to:
>   http://users.ox.ac.uk/~worc0337/authors/barbara.comyns.html
> Griffiths, P   *Sixty Glorious Years in Bidford-on-Avon*, 1993 (Brewin Books)
> [No author]   *The Morris Ring: Centenary of the Revival of the Shakespearean Bidford Morris,* 1986
> Spiers, A G F *Summary of the First 100 Years of the Parish Council of Bidford-on-Avon, 1894 -1994,* 1994
> Vernon-Wadley, P   *Synoptical History of Bidford,* 1903
> Ward, A W   *A Guide to Bidford-on-Avon and Neighbourhood,* 1903 *(Harry Collins)*

Articles:

Bird, V   'Bidford-on-Avon through the eyes of an artist', *Warwickshire and Worcestershire Life, (n.d.)*

Churchley, R   'The Ancient Corporation of Bidford-on-Avon: its place in the local economy c.1550- c.1850, *Warwickshire History,* Vol XIV, (6), Winter 2010/11

Martin, J M   'The Social and Economic Origins of the Vale of Evesham Market Gardening Industry', *Agricultural History Review,* Vol 33, 1985

Undergraduate Projects:

Uggerløse, E   'Local Planning, 1950 – 2008' (Project submitted as part of Community Engagement and Governance degree, University of Gloucester, 2008)

INDEX

People:

Places:

INDEX